VIDALIA ONIONS

A History of Georgia's State Vegetable

LEE LANCASTER

THE
History
PRESS

Published by The History Press
Charleston, SC
www.historypress.com

First published 2023

Manufactured in the United States

ISBN 9781467154932

Library of Congress Control Number: 2023940683

Notice: The information in this book is true and complete to the best of our knowledge. It is offered without guarantee on the part of the author or The History Press. The author and The History Press disclaim all liability in connection with the use of this book.

To my wife and children, Keri, Nate and Caroline.

Praise God from whom all blessings flow.

CONTENTS

CONTENTS

ACKNOWLEDGEMENTS

There is nothing on earth that compares to a Vidalia onion or a Vidalia onion farmer. It's not just in the soil. It's in their blood. Thank you to all of them for making this crop what it is. It's worth the fight to keep it alive, to keep it special and to keep it on the grocery store shelves.

Thanks to all the people who shared their lives, stories and pictures with me.

Thanks to Delbert Bland, Bob Stafford, Jimmy Grimes, Jason Deal, Andy Stanton, Happy Wyatt, Matthew Kulinski, Erin White, Nick Vassy, Jay Jones, Jody Redding, Tommy Butler, Aunt Jewell Durrence, Teri Hughes and the staff at the University of Georgia Tifton Campus, former Georgia Agriculture Commissioner Gary Black, Georgia Agriculture Commissioner Tyler Harper, Dan Bremer and AgWorks H2, Amy Carter from the UGA School of Veterinary Medicine, Alexa Britton and the Vidalia Onion Museum, Debbie Evans and the Vidalia Chamber of Commerce, the City of Vidalia, the Ocmulgee Regional Library, the Ladson Genealogical Library, the Glennville Public Library, Ray Farms of Glennville, B&B Farms of Cedar Crossing.

Thanks to Ms. Starks for teaching me how to read, Mrs. Long for teaching me how to write, Dr. Elder for teaching me how to write something people could read and Mama for making me go to school.

INTRODUCTION

Would an onion by any other name smell as sweet? There's a reason it's called a Vidalia onion. My apologies to those who came before who grew Tattnall Sweets, Toombs County Sweets and Glennville Sweets. The name is sweet. And ever since the beginning, it's been the best on the market, by far. It demands a higher price because it is worth more. From the onion's small start on the back of a wagon built from an old Model T Ford, Southeast Georgia now produces over $160 million worth of Vidalia onions annually. In a small area in Southeast Georgia where only about ten thousand acres of these special onions grow, the economic impact has grown to nearly $400 million.

There are thousands of recipes for Vidalia onions, and every way you cook them has the potential to be amazing, as long as you use the genuine article. But how can you be sure, and why do people make such a fuss over the name?

Vidalia onions are special. They taste better. There's no place on earth where they grow 'em any better. Ever since the first Vidalia onion was sold, there have been counterfeiters and pirates looking to make a killing passing off no-name onions for Vidalia's and thinking no one would notice. But the onion has an unbelievable fan base that can tell a fink a mile away.

How I love Vidalia onions! Let me count the days till they grace the shelf of my local grocery store. As I was researching this subject, I realized that only recipe books on Vidalia onions exist. But we need to know how and where we got Vidalia onions, too. Come dig in and read about a slice of one of Georgia's most famous and important crops.

THERE'S JUST SOMETHING
ABOUT THAT NAME

Vidalia. There's just something about that name. Since it was lent to a vegetable some years ago, it just whispers sweet. Do you know anybody named Vidalia? Probably not. Even if you did, she wouldn't be as sweet as a Vidalia onion. It seems to be the perfect mixture, a sweet onion and the sweet little town it grew up in. But it hasn't always been easy, and the road has been rough to get where it is. There's a legend that says when European explorers came through the area, they saw Native Americans eating onions like apples. That would make a great story if it was true.

Vidalia onions haven't been around that long; neither has the town they are named after. But when they were first discovered, they were addictive. The vegetable proved to be hard to grow but worth the trouble. Before the Vidalia onion, there was no such thing as a sweet onion, just onions. Pungent, strong, make you cry, stick with you till tomorrow, onions.

But first things first: you've gotta pronounce it right! There are two correct ways to say it, kinda like pecan and pecan, that must be used in two different settings. First of all, if you're addressing an audience of dignitaries from some other place or if you're talking to the president of the United States, you say "Vi-Dale-Yah." For the rest of us, if you're in Vidalia or talking about Vidalia to your cousin in Michigan, you say "Vi-Day-Yah." There ain't no *L* in Vidalia if you pronounce it right. Butchering the name won't get you anywhere. I've heard it pronounced many different wrong ways, the most frequent being "Va-Doll-Yah." I know y'all mean well, and we appreciate your business, but you gotta get it right before we can proceed any further.

The area around Vidalia had a similar beginning to all the other areas nearby. Huge pine trees were cut for lumber while others were tended to produce naval stores, or turpentine. Not much happened in the area until the SAM railroad line was formed and plotted a course through the middle of the area, connecting Savannah, Americus and Montgomery, Alabama, while trying to avoid the rivers. Cities were formed, and some became ghost towns in those days, because of the decisions made where railroads were laid and junctions connected. The decision for a railroad connection between Macon, Dublin and Savannah to be built where Vidalia would be founded, instead of Higgston to the west, proved to be the starting point for the city. Soon, other railroads found the area favorable and connected through the little unnamed place from seven different directions.

Most of the early settlers came to Vidalia from North Carolina, like most of the settlers in the communities around it. A man named Warren T. Jenkins traveled from Robeson County, North Carolina, to Mount Vernon. He met a man named Jim McNatt there and started a turpentine business with him. They decided to build a turpentine still at a place where they could easily load naval stores onto the train at a place ten miles east of Mount Vernon along the railroad bed, prior to the track being laid.

Since there weren't enough people living in the area at the time to effectively employ, Jenkins went back to North Carolina to hire more people to come work in his newly settled area. He needed some equipment and supplies, so he went through Savannah and ordered what he needed to be shipped to his company, Jenkins and McNatt. Since the railroad wasn't finished, the supplies were shipped by boat through the Intercoastal Waterway, up the Altamaha River, up the Oconee River to the landing west of Mount Vernon where the Highway 280 bridge is now and pulled by mules back to what was known as Jenkins Station. In honor of the man considered the town's founder, Warren T. Jenkins, the town was briefly known as Jenkins Station. Obviously, the name didn't stick. According to Jenkins's son, as the very first freight train pulled in after the railroad was completed, the conductor began to inquire where he was. "Is this Vidalia?" asked the conductor. Jenkins said, "I don't know. I've never heard of that name. Why do you ask?" The conductor answered, "I have a shipment of goods here for a firm named Jenkins and McNatt at Vidalia." Jenkins, part owner of Jenkins and McNatt, answered, "Well, I'm Jenkins, so I guess this must be Vidalia." Somebody had renamed the place and didn't bother to tell the residents!

Where the name Vidalia came from hasn't always been completely clear. It was believed the president of the SAM railroad, Sam Hawkins, named it after his daughter, which would have been sweet if it was true. In 1917, a local attorney wrote the history of how Vidalia got its name, and everybody took it as the gospel until somebody looked up Colonel Sam Hawkins's family tree and found an assumed limb missing. Printed in the 1983 book *Sumter County History* was the Hawkins family lineage outlined within its pages. Hawkins had four girls: Nancy Louise, Eva, Agnes and Cordelia. Not a one named, Vidalia. Not even a middle name. His wife wasn't named Vidalia either. She also was named Cordelia, and the colonel took the liberty of naming Cordele after his wife and daughter.

The story does have a little truth to it. One of Sam Hawkins's daughters, no one knows which one, rode in a passenger car along the length of the newly constructed rail line toward Montgomery and named all the unnamed stations for five dollars apiece. Some of the towns were inspired by the Hawkins family's recent trip to Europe, explaining where names like Lyons, Milan and Rhine came from. The daughter picked the name Vidalia without telling anybody why, but it is assumed that she was familiar with the city of Vidalia, Louisiana, some six hundred miles away and on the other side of the Mississippi River. That town's name was changed in 1811 in honor of its Spanish founder, Don Jose Vidal. Vidal is not someone you should be familiar with unless you live in Vidalia, Louisiana or maybe even Natchez, Mississippi, just across the river.

Vidalia city limits sign west side of town on U.S. Highway 280. *Author's collection.*

Giant polished Vidalia onion statue outside Vidalia Onion Committee office and entrance to Vidalia Onion Museum. *Author's collection.*

The city of Vidalia, Georgia, was officially named and incorporated in 1890. U.S. Highway 280 is the main street through Vidalia as well as Lyons, the county seat, next door. It was built as a connecting road split off from the main route out west, U.S. Highway 80. Highway 280 connects Fort Stewart in Hinesville and Fort Benning in Columbus, then continues on into Alabama. For much of its route, U.S. Highway 280 parallels the original SAM rail line that was laid in the nineteenth century.

When the city of Vidalia was founded, it was situated approximately five miles east of Higgston and five miles west of Lyons. Today, the western edge of the city of Vidalia extends to, if not into, Montgomery County and almost joins Higgston. Vidalia and Lyons share much of their border, which runs perpendicular to U.S. Highway 280.

The city of Vidalia has totally committed itself to its famous crop. The city's motto was changed from "City of Progress" to the "Sweet Onion City" when the Vidalia onion began to collect steam. The city's water tanks, including the one near the Recreation Department, has the city motto with sweet onions painted on both sides. A stainless-steel onion fountain sits along Highway 280 at City Park, a city event venue along the route into downtown Vidalia, while a similar sculpture graces the top of the new courthouse currently under construction in Lyons.

In 1972, Police Chief Robert Watson moved from Fort Valley to Vidalia. In Fort Valley, the peach industry is so huge that the state legislature named the county "Peach County" when it was formed in 1924. The Fort Valley police uniforms had a peach on their sleeve patches. When Chief Watson told Vidalia mayor Hugh Dixon about the patches, he made some phone calls and got Vidalia onions put on the Vidalia police sleeve patches. Just in the last few years, the City of Vidalia Police Department has also added

The City of Vidalia water tank near the Vidalia Recreation Department on U.S. Highway 280. *Author's collection.*

Top: Stainless-steel sweet onion structure atop new Toombs County Courthouse under construction at time of picture. *Author's collection.*

Middle: Stainless steel onion fountain at Vidalia City Park in downtown Vidalia. *Author's collection.*

Bottom: City of Vidalia police car. Note the onion on the side. *Author's collection.*

onions to the paint scheme of their patrol cars. No word as to whether onions are printed on their ticket books, though.

Some of the banks in town have onion plants incorporated into their logos out front. There are plywood onions hanging on street signs and lampposts throughout the county. Cars once sold by Vidalia Ford had sweet onions on the dealer stickers. If you want the onion feel without the new car smell, you can buy a used car from Sweet Onion City Motors. The local radio station for news, high school sports and talk radio is WVOP. I hate to bring tears to your eyes, but the Vidalia High School sports mascot is not the fighting onion, it's an Indian.

2

A TALE OF TWO COUNTIES

TOOMBS COUNTY

Fifteen years after Vidalia was founded, a new county was formed around it in 1905. Toombs County was cut from Montgomery County and named after Robert Toombs, the famous Georgia orator, senator, fireball and secretary of state of the Confederate States during the Civil War. The other small towns and communities in Toombs County are Santa Claus, Johnson's Corner, Cedar Crossing, Ohoopee, Stanleys Store, Blue Ridge and English Eddy.

The community of Santa Claus sits on U.S. Highway 1 below Lyons with its northern boundary marked by a city limit sign and a life-size Santa Claus statue. As you turn down Noel Street, you'll find city hall at 25 December Drive. In front of the office is a red mailbox that says "Santa's Mail," where Christmas cards are dropped off every year to get a special postmark from the city. The post office in Santa Claus is long gone, so the letters are then taken to the post office in Lyons for final delivery. The city of Santa Claus was founded in the 1930s by a farmer named Calvin Greene. He wanted to attract tourists to his pecan business on the newly built U.S. Highway 1. He carved out sixty acres of his pecan orchard for the city, which was incorporated in 1941. In the 1960s, Bill Salem developed the city by building most of the houses, water, sewage and roads. The streets in town were all named with Christmas themes, like Dasher, Dancer, Rudolph and Reindeer and one after Bill Salem. The

Top, left: Original hand-painted Santa Claus city limits sign displayed in Santa Claus Museum. *Author's collection.*

Top, right: Santa Claus postage stamp displayed in Santa Claus Museum. *Author's collection.*

Bottom: Twenty-plus-foot-tall Santa and Mrs. Claus stand in Cedar Crossing during the Christmas season. *Author's collection.*

biggest business in town is the John Deere tractor dealership, where lots of Vidalia onion farmers buy their farming equipment and parts. Vidalia onions can usually be seen growing within the city limits.

At a crossroads south of Highway 1 is the community of Cedar Crossing. Though it is a small crossroads on Highway 56 and lacks a post office, it is the epicenter of the Vidalia onion farming community in Toombs County.

Every day at noon, dozens of farmers and workers from onion farms throughout the region meet up at a little diner on the edge of an onion patch. Jan's Fried Chicken is the best place to catch lunch for miles around. Fried chicken, chicken fingers, shrimp, gizzards, sweet tea and pound cake are on the menu every day. Log trucks and delivery drivers stop in on the way and blend in with the dusty hat and boot crowd. When the onions are growing, travelers stop and snap pictures to share with family from the edge of the onion patch when they finish eating. During the season, the highway out front is lined with dried onion skins.

TATTNALL COUNTY

On the east side of the sandy, lazy creek called the Ohoopee River lies Tattnall County. It's a sandy, flat area dotted with agriculture communities and sawmills kept alive by a rural network of Dollar Generals. Among the sand beds and turkey oak stands are thousands of acres of Vidalia onion fields. Tattnall County is huge, stretching out an hour's drive between the Altamaha River in the south to almost touching Interstate 16 in the north. Tattnall County is home to several small farming communities: Collins, Cobbtown, Mendez and Goose Neck.

Several years ago, a spaceship was reported to have crash-landed in the middle of downtown Glennville, Tattnall County's largest city. After further investigation, it was a movie prop. Will Smith stayed in town for several weeks while filming the movie *Gemini Man* on sets spread out around the area.

Tattnall County was created in 1801, over one hundred years before Toombs County. The county was named after Josiah Tattnall, who was governor of Georgia at the time. He signed the bill that named the county after him when the state capital was in Louisville. At the time, there wasn't much civilization to speak of in the state, besides the area between Savannah and Augusta. A deal between the state and the Creek Nation created Washington County, a huge piece of land stretching between the Altamaha and Ogeechee Rivers, from present-day Lexington to an area south of Hinesville. It became impossible to govern, so it was cut into several pieces. Montgomery County was formed from the part along the Altamaha, with Tattnall formed from it a few years later. No plans were made for a county seat because no towns or communities were within the Tattnall County borders. In 1828, the state legislature passed a bill requiring a surveyor to determine the center of the county, marking where the courthouse and jail would be built. In 1832, the first post office was built in the county, and the city of Reidsville was named after Robert R. Reid, the superior court judge for the county. Reid moved to Florida afterward and was appointed territorial governor in the years before it officially became a state. Most early settling in the county was done along the Altamaha River. Because no roads existed, the river was the only way in or out of the county.

When the first roads in the county were built, most of them pointed to and from Savannah. When two roads crossed, a community sprang up. At a small settlement in the southern portion of the county, a two-story building was built by the Masonic Order. One floor was for lodge meetings, while the other floor was used as a public school. The community, known as Philadelphia Church at the time, hired a Baptist preacher named Glenn J. Thompson to teach at the school. As more people moved into the community, they requested a post office be built. For a post office to be built, the community needed to submit a list of suggested names. Glennville was suggested, to be named after their new preaching teacher. The post office in Glennville opened in 1889, with Glenn J. Thompson serving as its first postmaster.

Tattnall County is extremely flat, giving several glimpses of the tallest building in the county from miles away in the onion fields and cow pastures between Reidsville and the Altamaha. Rising from the junction of Highway 147 and 178, behind gray walls and razor wire, stands Georgia State Prison, once home to the state's original electric chair, putting away Georgia's most notorious criminals like John Wallace, the villain in *Murder in Coweta County*; Billy Sunday Burt, the hit man for the "Dixie Mafia"; and all four gang members responsible for the notorious Alday murders in Seminole County. The original *The Longest Yard* starring Burt Reynolds and Eddie Albert was filmed inside its walls. The site contains several thousand acres of cropland where corn, potatoes and beef cattle are produced and also includes a dairy and cannery. On a hill off Highway 178 stands a macabre, silent graveyard with no tombstones, only hundreds of white crosses marked with numbers. Somewhere under the clay are stored the prisoners who died inside the walls of the prison but were never claimed to be buried back home.

In the sand bed region, Brazell's Creek burns its way south through the flat woods and parallels the deep-cut run of the Ohoopee until it finally gives up its independence and confluences south of Reidsville. In the run of Brazell's Creek lies Jack Hill State Park, formerly Gordonia-Alatamaha State Park, and the Brazell's Creek Golf Course. The state park was recently

Georgia State Prison Boot Hill outside Reidsville. *Author's collection.*

renamed after the popular Reidsville businessman and long-serving state senator who died in office in 2020.

Back in 1945, Gene Armstrong caught a pile of crickets for fish bait and put them in an empty sugar barrel with sand in the bottom. Three weeks later, he looked in the barrel and found what he thought were ants eating the crickets. But when he looked closer, what he saw turned out to be baby crickets. An idea was hatched along with the crickets. Gene's father, Tal, learned how to grow crickets commercially. Then in 1947, Tal quit his job as a plumber to open Armstrong's Cricket Farm in Glennville. In 1954, Armstrong's expanded their operation by opening another farm in Louisiana. Later, they expanded their operation by selling other feeder insects, including mealworms, horn worms, wax worms and super worms. They supply the needs of not only fishermen but also scientists, pet shops, teachers and pet owners all across the country.

Glennville is also the hometown of two former NFL players, Sterling and Shannon Sharpe. The elder brother, Sterling, was Brett Favre's number one receiver at Green Bay before having his career cut short by a neck injury. Shannon won Super Bowls with the Denver Broncos and Baltimore Ravens. Both went on to have careers as commentators on ESPN.

Mural painting at Armstrong's Cricket Farm in Glennville. Paintings of past employees and the sugar barrel that started it all. *Author's collection.*

Like Toombs County, Tattnall missed the jackpot known as Interstate 16 when it was built. Also like Toombs County, a major U.S. highway was cut through the county as the main route to Florida when it was built. Nothing dampened the spirits of travelers through Glennville on their way to Miami until they came to the other end of the county and saw a Governor Lester Maddox–mandated sign warning motorists of the speed trap ahead in Ludowici. In Ludowici, inside the barbershop on the corner where 301 turned south, was a switch on the wall. That switch controlled the red light at the intersection where the police would be watching. It got the governor's attention, so he threatened to move the state capital to Long County until the town straightened up its act.

3

A MAN NAMED MOSE

The early twentieth century proved to be mighty rough for Georgia farmers. Most everybody grew cotton, as they had for the previous two hundred years. The Great War was still raging in Europe and created gigantic demand for cotton that drove the price over one dollar a pound. Profits were easy in those days, no matter what cotton cost to produce. There were over five million acres of "Georgia snow" planted in 1918, the year an invasive visitor from Mexico called the boll weevil crossed the state line into Georgia near Thomasville. Within eighteen months, the boll weevil had infested the entire state, all the way to the North Georgia mountains. Cotton yields were chewed in half, while farmers threw every chemical and powder they could find to try to slow it down. With this obstacle came an opportunity to explore other crops. Peanuts got their start in the state in the shadow of the boll weevil, as did a lot of vegetable crops that weevils couldn't eat.

According to a *Macon Telegraph* article from August 28, 1919,

Many of the businessmen of this city, among them W.O. Donovan, E.L. Meadows, George N. Matthews, J.W. McWhorter, George S. Rountree, W.T. McAuthur, Sr., and others are interested in the project of a market here for everything the farmer grows, and plans are being now worked out to provide the market. The farmers are ready to quit cotton and will gladly turn their attention to other things. The boll weevil has given them a thorough drubbing this year and they are ready to plant almost anything in place of cotton.

In response to the boll weevil, the State of Georgia created the University of Georgia Extension Service to better serve farmers through county agents armed with new information from studies and laboratory work done at the College of Agriculture in Athens. The first county agent for Toombs County was a man named C.G. Gardner. He helped local farmers in a little crossroads community below Lyons called Johnson's Corner start growing sweet potatoes instead of cotton. They stuck with it and were soon growing more sweet potatoes than any other county in the country.

In 1921, J.G. Duncan of Elizabeth City, North Carolina, came to Johnson's Corner to visit his son, W.L. Duncan, a Nazarene preacher in the community. They tried to start slips (vine cuttings planted in a bed to produce plants) from seed but found the seed material had a hard time making the trip from sweet potato country to Southeast Georgia. Finally, they prevailed and distributed slips to farmers around the area, who planted about eight thousand slips per acre. The farmers produced enough of a crop to fill a train boxcar, with a carload bringing $1,500. At about the same time, another group tried, and failed, to grow sweet potatoes around Quitman. The next year, Reverend Duncan bought a farm to grow sweet potatoes, and the group of farmers grew enough to fill 3 boxcars. In the following year, 1923, the farmers produced 6 boxcars worth, followed by 22.5 in 1924. In 1925, they filled 110 cars. At the time, growers were making $200 per acre on yams. In 1926, they tallied up $250,000 worth of Big Stem Jersey and Porto Rican variety yams.

In the 1920s, sweet potato farming started in January with bed preparation. Planting was done in late March or early April. Digging Big Stem Jerseys started around July 10, and the Porto Rican variety matured a week earlier, around July 2.

There was also another crop starting to be produced in Toombs County in the early 1920s, according to an article in the July 7, 1923 edition of the *Atlanta Tri-Weekly Journal*:

> *The first shipment of onions went from this county Monday when W.O. Donovan shipped several crates to Atlanta. Several other farmers have onions to ship from around Vidalia and it is expected that a total express shipment will go during the next few weeks of about a carload. Mr. Donovan is so well pleased with the yield that he says he will plant 50 acres in them for next spring.*

W.O. Donovan was well known throughout Toombs County. He was originally from Wadley, before moving to Macon and then Vidalia. His expertise was in lumber and turpentine, and he also served as a county commissioner for his area and mayor pro tem of the city of Vidalia in the 1910s and 1920s. He was a founding partner in a casket manufacturer in Savannah, partner in one of the railroads and president of the First National Bank of Vidalia. There is no word whether the Bermuda onions he grew in 1923 were sweet, with no mention of his production later on. In 1925, he and his family moved to Ocala, Florida, where he became president of a lumber company. He was killed changing a flat tire on a trip back from Daytona beside the road one night in 1928. The family returned to Vidalia to reside shortly after his death.

In 1944, the sweet potato crop in Toombs County was touted as the most valuable in the area. The acreage was increased by over 1,000 from the previous year to a total of 4,500. The average yield of sweet potatoes per acre was about 150 bushels in all grades, with a bushel weighing 55 pounds. Bringing $3 per bushel for #1s, the crop was expected to bring in about $1.5 million that year.

The farmers organized the Toombs County Sweet Potato Grower's Association and, according to an article in the *Macon Telegraph*, first "appointed a manager who was not at heart in sympathy with cooperatives and that retarded their development until M.M. Coleman Jr. was selected as manager." M.M. Coleman Jr. later served the association as its president also. He was also known as Mose Coleman.

Mose Coleman was a well-rounded farmer who tended a farm between Lyons and Vidalia. His father, M.M. Coleman Sr., was described as a farmer who liked to explore new crops and try to establish them in Toombs County. In 1908, he planted the very first pecan orchard in the county on about three acres. His son, Mose, tended the orchard, harvested the nuts and shipped his pecan crop to Albany to be marketed. Mose Jr.'s flock of leghorn chickens won several livestock judging and production awards in the 1920s. He produced his own layer feed and sold to other farmers. He and nearby farmers produced enough eggs to establish egg shipments to Florida by rail on the Seaboard Railway line. He grew cotton and tomatoes and had several tenants grow cotton and sweet potatoes on some of his property.

Mose Coleman decided to experiment with some new crops: "It began in the fall of 1930. I was getting up my seed order, and my wife, Alice, was helping me. I had been trying things such as spinach, and lettuce, and asparagus, and when I saw the ads for onions in the catalogue, I wondered why people in Georgia didn't grow them. I decided I couldn't go wrong with a few so I placed the order," he told the *Vidalia Advance* in 1979. The original onion seeds he ordered were Crystal Wax Bermuda, a white onion variety. These onions could be planted in mid- to late fall and harvested before the sweet potato land was to be prepared again in May. He ordered a few onion seeds and planted them with a seed drill. He grew about a quarter acre of onions on the plot of land where the Walmart now sits on Highway 280 east of downtown Vidalia. When the onions sprouted, he thinned the stand with a hoe to give them space. The onions did extraordinarily well, growing big and "shiny as if they had been polished with wax." What he had grown was a whole new vegetable—the sweet onion!

That quarter acre of onions created a problem for Coleman: he had too many! The family could only eat so much, no matter how good the onions were. He needed to harvest them and store what his family didn't eat in the smokehouse. When the smokehouse was full, he still had a pile left. The Depression was in its beginning stages, and not many grocery stores existed. Most stores were usually out in the country, owned by one person: the one stocking, cleaning, ordering stock items, filling orders and generally running the place. The beautiful, shiny onions were a hard sell because the store owners feared they wouldn't store long enough to sell. Since money was tight, everybody wanted to squeeze every penny they could.

If Mose Coleman was going to sell the rest of his onion crop before it spoiled, he'd have to sell them outside of town. So he built a wagon made out of the bed of a Model T Ford to pull behind his car and hit the road. After a lot of hard bargaining, he sold the rest of his crop. The going price for the sweet onions was $3.50 for a fifty-pound sack. The Depression had depressed the prices of every other commodity. In the same *Vidalia Advance* article, Coleman said, "At that time, cotton was almost nothing. Hogs were as low as 2 cents per pound and cows were selling for 3 or 4 cents per pound. Those onion prices were mighty encouraging to me for I had raised, picked and sold butterbeans for 1 cent per pound and cabbage for just $20 a ton." In spite of the difficulty unloading his produce, he increased his acreage to two and a half acres the following year. "With the Depression on, other farmers couldn't get enough to pay for their fertilizer. They all thought I had found a gold mine." In 1932, with the help of their county agent, E.P. Drexel, farmers organized a depot on Highway 1 in Lyons. They could fill a passing truck with corn, butter beans and white Bermuda onions.

The third year Coleman grew onions, other area farmers grew onions too. In time, he started using vertical integration. He supplied the plants and fertilizer to farmers while they tended the onions and harvested them. When the onions were sold, Coleman and the farmers split the profit. Lots

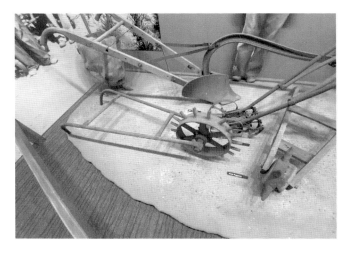

Antique onion farming tools displayed. Mostly horse-drawn equipment. Original onion pegger in foreground. *Vidalia Onion Museum.*

of farmers jumped on board and replaced the crops they couldn't make money from with onions. In 1940, Mose grew two hundred acres of white and yellow onions on a cooperative basis. Seeds came from the Iberian Peninsula, seed beds were planted in late summer, and the onion plants was transplanted in late November. There was an onion expert who worked with the farmers in those days named J.H. McNeil. That year had a larger supply of onions and competition from other farmers, so the prices fell to $1 or $2 per bag. Compared to everything else, plenty of money was to be made at that price. The total income expected from growing onions in 1940 was around $20,000.

Coleman grew his business and made changes to be more profitable. Instead of buying seed, drilling them and thinning the stand, he bought seedlings from the Rio Grande Valley for sixty cents per thousand. Hand-planting live plants, similar to how the farmers grew tobacco, made a strong stand. Another change he made was to start using a yellow Bermuda onion instead of the Crystal Wax because it stored better and tasted the same.

Once his orders were fulfilled around home, Coleman rented a shed on the State Farmer's Market in Columbia, South Carolina, to get better prices for his onions. When U.S. Highway 1 opened, he hauled loads all the way to the markets in Philadelphia, Pennsylvania.

Prior to his venturing into the onion business, Coleman had dealt produce to the local A&P store in Vidalia. The store had to close because of the Depression, but the store's manager, Mr. Paulk, had been put in charge of the stores in Augusta and South Carolina. Coleman went to see Paulk and took a bag of sweet onions with him. In Paulk's office, Coleman sliced an onion up like an apple, ate a piece and handed a piece to the manager. The onions Paulk was used to eating were way too strong to try a trick like that. The taste test worked! Paulk wrote a letter for Coleman to show all A&P store managers that said they had to buy their onions from him and no one else until he ran out.

The 1946 season was a tough one for the fledgling industry. A local plant dealer brought in a trailer load of onion plants from Texas, with a total of over 40 million plants delivered to the area for planting. The number of sweet onions planted swelled to about 1,200 acres, with the average farm growing about 8. The expected yield was around 10,000 pounds per acre. Even though the world war was over, the economy still wasn't good. And as the gigantic harvest rolled in, the onion market was saturated and the onions sat and rotted. The produce buyer for Tanner-Brice, a local grocery wholesaler, bought all the onions he could for twenty-five cents per bag. Though his price was one-tenth of what the farmers expected, they had no choice. Most of the farmers in the onion business at that time got out and never grew onions again. That episode stuck with the local farmers for decades and put Toombs County onions on hiatus until the 1970s.

When Coleman was asked about his role in the discovery of the sweet onion, he told this story:

> *About five years ago, I was in Comanjilla, Mexico, which is a hot spring in Mexico, taking a hot bath. I overheard two men near me talking. One was from North Georgia and the other was from Oklahoma. The one from Georgia was telling the one from Oklahoma that he should try some Vidalia onions because they were the best onions produced. To be that far from home and to hear my town and its onions praised that way made me feel mighty good.*

4

ED TENSLEY AND

THE GLENNVILLE TOMATO

While Toombs County was becoming the sweet potato capital, Glennville was establishing itself as "Georgia's largest tomato market." The crop was popular with travelers along Highway 301, with a farmers market situated in town with a giant tomato marking the entrance. The original market was at the corner of Highway 301 and Hencart Road, near where the Rusty Pig now sits. The Georgia State Farmers Market was moved to its current location south of town in 1936, with the giant tomato making the move as well.

Tomatoes and other nursery plants for transplanting were grown in large quantities in Tattnall County. In the Tison community, the Beasley Farm produced 80 acres of tomato plants for many years. When the Glennville Farmers Market was moved in 1936, there were 2,500 acres of tomatoes grown with four packing sheds and a tomato cannery in town to move them into the shipping channels. Six thousand bushels of Bermuda onions were grown and sold locally that year.

A big part in the establishment of the farming industry in Glennville was an African American man named E.S. Tensley. His six-hundred-acre farm was located where the Glennville Recreation Department now stands. The pond near the recreation department was dug to irrigate the Tensley farm. Edmund Samuel Tensley was born in North Carolina on August 9, 1895. He served in World War I and assumedly trained at the facility known as Camp Dix before fulfilling his duty in the war effort. He must have liked the area because he moved to nearby Browns Mill, New Jersey, after being discharged and studied agriculture at postsecondary school near there. In 1937, he farmed with a partner in the Crosswicks area. In the 1940s, he moved to Glennville and met Thelma Alston, whom he married in 1946. Thelma helped by managing the business side of the farming operation. Because Thelma liked to fish, the irrigation pond E.S. Tensley dug was kept stocked with fish.

"I can tell you, Ed Tensley was the first man to ever plant onions or tomatoes in Glennville. I had moved to Charlotte, North Carolina when I first heard the name Vidalia sweet onion, and I was so mad because I knew better. Those were Glennville onions brought there by Ed Tensley!" Altha Bynum told the *Glennville Sentinel* in 2007. Tensley started out farming with several mules, showed others how to rotate crops and was the first farmer to use a tractor in Tattnall County. "He is certainly the one who brought sweet onions here," said Ruben King Sr. King started out working for Tensley at one dollar per hour, which was unheard back then. He worked on the farm for several years and opened King and Sons Funeral Home in Glennville in 1966.

Ed Tensley grew 250 acres of tomato plants outside Glennville in 1942. That acreage produced 11 million Marglobe and Rutgers tomato plants for distribution in New Jersey, Virginia, Pennsylvania and Maryland. He delivered tomato plants, grown from seed certified by the Georgia Department of Agriculture, to a warehouse in Crosswicks, south of Trenton, New Jersey. He advertised the plants at the warehouse were dug in Glennville and delivered to Crosswicks in ventilated trucks, sometimes promised within twenty-four hours. The tomato plants were packed in moss harvested from the Okefenokee Swamp near Folkston to keep them moist on the long ride north. His farm also produced 18 acres of tomatoes and 50 acres of snap beans to market in town or elsewhere if the price didn't hold. He also grew California wonder bell pepper plants for shipping, watermelons, tobacco, cotton, corn, peanuts and 5 acres of onions.

Ed Tensley told the *Glennville Sentinel* in May 1942 that unless it rained, he'd only be able to ship about another three million plants that season. In the 1940s and '50s, E.S. Tensley grew tomato and tobacco plants for the farmers around Glennville on thirty acres in Florida. The orders were taken in December at the Western Union Office and sold by Tattnall Plant Farm, with tomatoes arriving in early March and tobacco later in the month. Tattnall Plant Farm also began to receive onion transplants from Texas.

Thelma and Ed Tensley had no children but adopted their niece, Ann. She told the *Glennville Sentinel* about her father:

He bought the first school bus for the black kids and when orange season was in in Florida, he'd buy cases of them and give to the schools for their lunches. If they needed basketball or baseball uniforms at the black school, he'd buy them. If anyone came to him from the school system and said they needed something, he'd give it to them. He was highly educated and always promoted it with my cousins and other family members. He wanted to be sure everyone could read and had a good education.

Tensley's niece added, "He was all about business. He taught us to never use credit cards and to keep good credit. He'd say that if you couldn't afford it, then don't charge it. Wait and save up for it. He was always trying to find some business to make money. He made money, spent money, and enjoyed the riches of life." Ed Tensley loved baseball more than anybody around town. Every year when the World Series was played, Tensley traveled north to attend every game. This was during the time when the series was centralized, before the Dodgers and Giants moved to California.

Tensley was a good row crop farmer as well. Over the years, he was trusted with the planting and tending of large tracts of cotton for several nearby farmers, including Segal Durrence of Reidsville. Tensley's daughter explained his role in starting the sweet onion industry in the area: "At the time, the onion was known as the Georgia sweet onion and then later Dad went to Vidalia and taught them how to grow it too."

On November 25, 1972, E.S. Tensley died, followed by Thelma in 2007. His obituary in the local paper read as follows:

He will be remembered for the wonderful contributions he brought and shared with the farmers of Tattnall County and adjacent counties and the many jobs he provided for people—both black and white—that they might make a decent livelihood. He had compassion and tried to meet the needs of the individual regardless of race, color or creed. He has a deep concern for developing and fostering the course of education in Tattnall County. He bought and furnished the first school bus for the transportation of black boys and girls to the Glennville Junior High School. Thank God for giving us the man, Ed Tensley.

5

THE VIDALIA STATE FARMERS MARKET
AND EARLIE ADOPTERS

In the 1940s, the discovery of the sweet onion in Toombs County got the attention of the Georgia commissioner of agriculture Tom Linder. After the first planting of less than an acre in 1930, there were reports of 1,200 acres of live plants set in 1946. Fifty thousand plants were set out per acre in those days. The onion business also had the attention of the governor of Georgia. Herman Talmadge lived in Lovejoy at the time, but his father, Eugene, had moved to Mount Vernon, near Vidalia, to start his law practice, where he later married his widowed secretary. The family moved to Telfair County, where they started Sugar Creek Plantation, and Gene ran for agriculture commissioner and eventually governor.

In 1949, local state representatives and Commissioner Linder persuaded the governor to approve the Department of Agriculture's budget, which included two dozen new state farmers' markets, including one in Vidalia. The fourteen-acre plot of land purchased for the market was located between Vidalia and Lyons. The market had frontage on Highway 280 and stretched to what was known as the Old Vidalia Highway. It also had frontage on the Seaboard Railroad. Construction included adding a spur for the rail line. The planned structure was to be two hundred feet long by sixty feet wide, with electrical, water and telephone service. Construction started near the beginning of October 1949 and was completed around January 15, 1950. The market was also equipped with an onion grading machine.

The first manager of the Vidalia State Farmer's Market was Frank Musselwhite from Cordele. He had been assisting his brother, Horace, in the management of the Cordele State Farmer's Market at the time of his promotion.

The Vidalia State Farmers' Market was dedicated on May 18, 1950, with Moultrie being dedicated the following Saturday. At the dedication ceremony, Agriculture Commissioner Linder stood on the flat concrete platform surrounded by bags of onions. He told the crowd of about 250, "There is no place in the country with as many advantages and as few disadvantages as Georgia." A demonstration of the onion grader was held after the commissioner's speech. The dedications of the Vidalia and Moultrie markets made the front page of the *Georgia Farmers' and Consumers' Market Bulletin* the next week.

In his front-page editorial in the *Market Bulletin*, Commissioner Linder stated:

> *Each Farmers' Market that is built is but a link in the chain. Last week, contracts were let for initial buildings at Sylvania and Waynesboro. A contract for the initial building at Thomson, will be let as soon as the bids can be received, and we expect to assume State control of the market, at Augusta, within sixty days.*
>
> *Markets will soon be in operation at Leesburg, Donalsonville, and Columbus and this gives the State a chain of markets reaching entirely across the State from Savannah to the Chattahoochee, and extending as far North as Toccoa and Rome, making a total number of twenty-five markets.*
>
> *As fast as possible we are putting in large truck scales for the convenience of the farmers, truckers and merchants on these markets. And, in a very short while we will begin to install a teletype system which will provide instantly up-to-the-minute information, on the market, to farmers and buyers as to prices prevailing all over the country.*

Commissioner Linder returned to the market in Vidalia a few days later to witness the opening of okra season. The okra came from Toombs and Appling Counties, with the first delivered from a farm in Surrency. The okra was bought by two local grocery distributors in town: Piggly Wiggly and Morris Food Stores. Many different crops were handled at the market, including watermelons, snap beans, tomatoes, squash, potatoes and cucumbers. During the winter of 1951, there was a twice-a-month poultry auction established at the market on Wednesday afternoons. Tomatoes began selling at the market very quickly, with a young produce buyer named Kenneth New frequenting the establishment.

When news came that a new market would be established in Vidalia, the farmers in the area increased their onion acreage in response. During the next year's planting season, the acreage of onions planted was increased again by 150 acres. The new market had caught the attention of Brand Brothers Produce, a produce company operating out of the Atlanta State Farmers Market in Forest Park and also the largest onion handlers in the world. They paid for the additional acres to be planted and planned to market the onions themselves in 1951.

The first onions to be delivered for the 1951 season were from Jeff Davis County. The load contained fifty-one bags, with another five hundred being harvested for delivery later. Yields of onions were expected to be two hundred fifty-pound bags per acre. There were three classes—1, 2 and 3—depending on damage and abnormalities. Onions were planted to grow to sizes jumbo and boiler. Boiler would be considered a medium today.

W.E. "Earlie" Jordan began to handle onion plants in cooperation with the Brand Brothers in the early 1950s from his business, the Toombs County Plant Corporation. He sold improved onion seedlings that were started in Texas, including Bermuda varieties in both yellow and white. The varieties Jordan sold were 986 yellow Bermudas, 690 white Bermudas and Granex Hybrid. Jordan also spoke at organized meetings with other farmers throughout the state that were interested in the onion business.

The Brand Brothers Produce Company handled different types of produce but kept onions year-round. They bought and sold onions from throughout the United States and Mexico. The onions they were accustomed to handling were western onions from Texas that had a long shelf life. The sweet onions from Georgia couldn't hold up as long as other onions because their sugar content caused them to rot very quickly. The onions often rotted before they made it to their destination, making the Brands sour on the crop and pull their support after several consecutive extremely wet winters in the mid-1950s destroyed the onion crops. The weather deflated the hopes of the farmers and caused them to again abandon onions as a crop. Very few onions were grown in the region for many years after the massive failures during that time. The Brand Brothers lost a lot of money and decided to leave the region. They moved part of their operations out to Hidalgo County, Texas, to grow their own onions and other produce on both sides of the Rio Grande.

The Brands joined another partner later on to grow and broker produce under the name Griffin and Brand Farms. Othal Brand became mayor of McAllen, Texas, in the 1970s and clashed with striking farmers with the

American Agriculture Movement in March 1978. Farmers were protesting the importation of inferior produce coming in from Mexico. The onions on the produce trucks that were stopped by the farmers were owned and bagged by Brand Brothers. Brand Brothers continued to operate out of the Atlanta market for many more years as well as operating packing houses in Texas.

A World War II veteran and longtime agribusinessman named Charles "Pinky" McRae owned Lyons Cotton and Fertilizer Company with his brother, James. McRae earned the nickname "Pinky" while playing high school basketball. Apparently, he had pink-tinted skin that showed itself well during his games. He began to sell onion plants at his warehouse, calling them "Sweet Toombs County Onions" in 1963. He had heard them called "Vidalia onions" because of their origins at the state farmers' market but thought they needed to be called "Toombs County onions" and "Toombs County Sweets" because they grew in the county and not in the city. McRae had a man named Van Lewis grow fifty acres of onions for him. Lewis was a good farmer from the small community of Blue Ridge near the Tattnall County line on Highway 152, not the town in North Georgia. After selling plants for a while, McRae found himself in the onion grading, buying and selling business. At his fertilizer warehouse, Pinky labeled his bags "Grown, Packed and Shipped by Lyons Cotton & Fertilizer Company." In the early 1970s, horrible weather again destroyed the onion crops for several years. The winters of 1969 and 1970 saw freezes kill about 90 percent of the onions those seasons. That disaster caused a lot of farmers to bow out, which left McRae and Piggly Wiggly Southern as the only large-quantity onion handlers around.

The Vidalia State Farmers' Market had begun to lose its influence in the region and never regained its footing after the wet weather in the 1950s and after the Brand Brothers left. The misfortune of the early 1970s proved to be the end of the farmers' market. Farmers and businesses rented out the shed for a couple of years until it was sold to the City of Vidalia and torn down in 1975.

6

A SOUTHERN PIG MEETS

THE VIDALIA ONION

Everything has its humble beginnings, even Piggly Wiggly. The chain of southern grocery stores was once the most prolific and successful company in the state. There were Piggly Wiggly's in what seemed like every South and Middle Georgia county, and several covered Macon. It was founded in the city of Vidalia, where it rose to become the biggest grocery chain in the state. Then it disappeared from the books in just over fifty years.

In turn-of-the-twentieth-century Georgia, there were few chain stores and no "grocery" stores. The Model T was scarce in South Georgia, as were paved roads. Roadbuilding here wasn't seriously undertaken until the Eugene Talmadge era between the world wars. Stores were locally owned and operated by a single proprietor. Customers who needed items would have to buy them by the pound and by the sack. Flour, sugar and farm supplies were ordered or given to the operator on a list, like Ike Godsey's place on the Waltons.

To resupply a store, oftentimes the owner would have to get stock from a feed mill, gristmill or lumber mill or make a trip to a supply warehouse in Savannah or Macon, on a long, hard unpaved road a world away from town. The proprietor wouldn't make the trip but maybe once a month or longer depending on the distance. Sugar, salt, tobacco, leather supplies and plows had to be purchased in bulk from quite a way off. Before refrigeration, country folks didn't buy meat from the store. They'd buy salt and sugar to cure meat that was raised and butchered on the farm and then preserved in the smokehouse.

C.F. Hays Store in downtown Musella, Georgia. *Author's collection.*

Stores were various sizes, depending on the amount of business. In town, the stores were on Main Street with glass windows and even electric lighting. In the country, tiny stores with dirt floors dotted the roads. Most had no electricity, which didn't get supplied in most rural Georgia places until after World War II. These stores were tiny but still served as a lifeline for country folks when they needed supplies. These places had front porches that served as the community meeting spot.

In the city of Vidalia, there was a man named Mitch Brice who had an idea to supply the good folks throughout Southeast Georgia. His father-in-law, E.L. Tanner, had previous experience in the wholesale business and helped Brice get established. Tanner visited several tiny country stores and talked them into letting him supply them with whatever they sold; he would make the trip to the big city and get the supplies in large quantities to be distributed out from Vidalia. With that, the Tanner-Brice Company was established in 1919. The company's purpose: "The principal business to be carried on by said corporation is that of dealing in wholesale and retail groceries, dry goods, and merchandise generally."

Most of the items the Tanner-Brice Co. handled were for farm use: crop seed, animal feed and so on. Dealing largely with a farming community, Tanner regularly traded food and supplies for farm products like milk and

Inside C.F. Hays Store in downtown Musella, Georgia. *Author's collection.*

eggs, called bartering. Good ol' fashion credit was also used to pay for items. When the Great Depression hit, the company became the owner of several of its customers' stores due to their inability to cover their bills. As the stores came under Tanner-Brice ownership, the company ran them and sent out supervisors to keep the network running. The first store the company took over was run by a man named Mr. Sims, so instead of continuing on under the names of a dozen previous owners, the newly acquired stores were rebranded as "Sims Stores." While the Depression ground along, Brice didn't run out of money, but the banks that supplied him with credit did. He decided it was time to leave the grocery business and continued with his less demanding, more promising investments, including Brice Cinemas, PAL Theatres and, since the introduction of the Model T, several Shell gas stations.

A young man in the area who heard of Brice's need to sell out was a salesman named Phil Friese. He had friends in a firm in New York called the Schroder Trust Company, which basically bought failing companies, split them up and sold the pieces for a profit. The Tanner-Brice Company at the time contained seventy-six stores, mostly Sims', and a warehouse in Vidalia with a combined annual sales total of $1.5 million. Investors bought in and divided up the investments, giving Brice a controlling interest in the Shell stations. On July 15, 1941, Brice attended his last meeting with Tanner-Brice and left the company for good.

Friese was named manager of the Tanner-Brice Company, and one of his first acts was to talk several farmers into growing sweet onions in the Toombs County area. Texas was the biggest supplier of onions and had a terrible yield in 1941. Friese presold onions all over the place and made an investment of $35,000 in the form of onion bags. But due to bad weather in the spring of 1942 and better weather in Texas, the onions didn't get moved before they rotted. The farmers were on the hook for the $35,000 worth of unused onion bags. The disintegrating onions were stacked in a pile thirty feet high that could be detected all the way to the county line. Luckily for Friese, there was a war brewing in the Pacific, so he jumped on the first train he found and didn't touch the ground until he was in California. He joined the army and served as a supply officer until the end of the war. When it was over, he decided not to take the same train home.

The next leader of the company was a man named H.B. "Hugo" Meyer. He decided the best way to run the company was to let the local folks make the decisions instead of sending out-of-towners to come in and make more mistakes than miracles. He also made a call to a friend of his that had worked on Wall Street for eight years after graduating from the University of Washington. He suggested this friend, G.H. "Gerry" Achenbach, move from New York City to Vidalia, Georgia, in the middle of World War II and run a wholesale grocery company, a business he knew nothing about. He thought about it for a while and came to Georgia, though he didn't plan on sticking around but just long enough to straighten out the company and move on to better things after he'd lengthened his résumé.

In the beginning, Achenbach had the same idea as the original investors: buy a company that's about to go under, work to get it back up and running, then sell it for a profit. After meeting the people working there and seeing how much they put into the company, he changed his mind. One of the people who met Achenbach when he first arrived, George Garrett, remembered him fondly:

> Gerry kind of surprised us at first when he came to town wearing a big Homburg hat. We thought he was ready to bring the law and the gospel to the Georgia Crackers. But then he got us together and this is what he said: "Boys, I want you to understand that I don't know a thing about the grocery business, you do, and I want you to tell me about it. But I do know how a business should be run. I'll keep the books straight if you'll help me

call the shots. Then if this company succeeds, it won't be my success. It will be our success. To boil it down it is very simple: practice the golden rule with everyone the company deals with: the employees, the suppliers, the stockholders, and most of all, the customers."

The business changed its focus from wholesale grocery to the retail stores when it stopped servicing stores that weren't owned by Brice-Tanner. The company expanded its selection by sending trucks to locations in South Carolina, Atlanta and Jacksonville, Florida, that could supply them with livestock feed, fresh meat, fruits and vegetables. Achenbach told Hugo Meyer his future plans for the company: "What I have in mind after the war is this: the whole trend of merchandising is toward self-service super stores." There was a new company out of Memphis, Tennessee, that was turning the retail industry inside out and had caught Achenbach's eye. He told Hugo Meyer in 1943, "I am about ninety percent convinced that we should take on a few Piggly Wiggly franchises. Frankly, I think they can teach us country boys so much about merchandising and how to run a chain of grocery stores that we would be foolish not to try them out." Clarence Saunders, the founder of Piggly Wiggly, was in the grocery business when he had an idea. The original country store format was still being used in big stores in large cities where the customer went to the clerk to place their order. If there were fifteen people in line, they would have to wait til the previous fourteen customers' orders were filled before their turn came. Saunders had the idea of letting customers inside the storage room, so to speak, and pick out the items they wanted. Then they would take their selections to the clerk to have them rung up. It was a brilliant idea that no one had ever thought of before. The idea took root and is now the basic format for every retail store in the world. No more waiting in line behind the Baldwin sisters at Ike Godsey's store to get a can of peaches! As to the origin of the name Piggly Wiggly, Saunders never clarified. He believed that not telling where the name came from added to the uniqueness of the brand.

The reasons for joining the Piggly Wiggly franchise were explained by Achenbach in 1943:

Operating in a rural area, we are isolated from the large highly competitive cities where companies thrive only by being as good as, or better than, the best. We needed teaching because we had no way of learning by observation. A small chain of food stores is handicapped purely because of its size. It lacks the volume buying power of the nation-wide chains.

It cannot afford separate advertising and merchandising departments. It cannot maintain a real estate department to analyze and select the most favorable store locations. It cannot bear the expense of architects who are specialists in designing and equipping stores. Association with the Piggly Wiggly Corporation can give us the advantages of bigness, and at the same time we can enjoy the benefits accruing to a small compact organization where direction is by personal influence rather than protocol.

The Brice-Tanner Company joined Piggly Wiggly in 1943 but didn't officially change its name to Piggly Wiggly Southern until 1961. The original line for the franchise was nearly the Fall Line through Georgia but was moved to encompass the entire state after a time.

The first Sims' store converted to a Piggly Wiggly occurred in 1943, at the store in Americus. That store had only been open for about four years. The first new Piggly Wiggly opened by the company was in Waynesboro that same year. The Waynesboro store opening didn't go completely according to plan, according to a letter from Achenbach to Hugo Meyer: "The Piggly Wiggly opening in Waynesboro went off quite smoothly except that our shelving trim was lost by the freight company, our checkout stands were uncompleted, and our sign painter got drunk and we had to put a brush in Strick's (Lucius Strickland) hand and have him paint the signs."

Things began to look up for the company, and it was rewarded with a front-page story in the Piggly Wiggly newsletter *The Turnstile* in 1944:

VIDALIA, GA.,—As this New Year begins, the food outlook in this city far surpasses that of any previous year, due to the fact that there's a sparkling new and modern Piggly Wiggly store just opened, ready and equipped to serve the people with the finest foods available.

This highly successful opening marked the fifth Piggly Wiggly store which the Sims organization has brought to the people of this section of the Cracker State. The new Vidalia Piggly Wiggly is one of the prettiest stores in the entire South situated in the hometown of the Sims Service Stores organization, every effort to make it the unusually modern, beautiful and convenient shopping center, which it is, was put forth by G.H. Achenbach, president of Sims Service Stores, and his group of loyal and efficient assistants.

The company found there was a problem in 1946 when it realized none of the store managers had any training in accounting. A man from outside the company, an accountant named J.A. "Jimmy" Crockett, was hired to remedy the problem. The biggest concern was the entire company had made over $3 million in grocery sales that year but only profited around $5,000!

After World War II was settled out, Piggly Wiggly Southern set out to expand in Middle Georgia. The original Piggly Wiggly Company out of Memphis had led J. Holland Brown and M.E. Everitt to establish stores in Macon, increasing their number to six by the time Tanner-Brice purchased them in December 1947. In 1954, S&H Green Stamps were made available for the first time at all Piggly Wiggly–Sims stores. That same year, the Tanner-Brice Company changed its name to Piggly Wiggly Sims Stores Inc. It would then officially become Piggly Wiggly Southern Inc. seven years later.

In 1952, the company moved to its new office in downtown Vidalia. But in 1963, the company decided to build one big, centralized warehouse and office complex in town to replace the nine separate storage buildings scattered all over downtown. In 1967, the new office building and giant warehouse was completed with a huge refrigerated section containing sixty-five thousand square feet of frozen storage.

In the early 1960s, Piggly Wiggly started purchasing onions from surrounding farmers. Nobody knew quite what to call them. First, they were called plain old "Vidalia Georgia Onions," then simply "Vidalia Onions." Finally, as sales exploded, they were called "Piggly Wiggly's Famous Vidalia Onions." Frank Fountain, produce buyer for the company, was a major influential factor in getting into and expanding the sweet onion business on both sides. He was able to convince several farmers to grow onions for the grocery chain and build the onion's name and reputation.

In June 1975, G.H. Achenbach stepped down from running the Piggly Wiggly Southern Company that he had helmed for thirty-three years but would continue as the chairman of the board of directors. He later helped develop personal finance curriculum for Georgia high school juniors and

Dublin Piggly Wiggly remains in the style of the original stores. *Author's collection.*

seniors to help them better understand money and the monetary system. Achenbach's successor at Piggly Wiggly Southern was Ronald Frost from Wrightsville. His father, Roy Frost, had served as vice president in the company and worked there for forty years. The younger Frost worked his way up in the company after starting out part time at sixteen years old while working at the Wrightsville Piggly Wiggly when his father was the manager.

In 1984, there were 123 Piggly Wiggly stores in Georgia, with 82 owned and operated by Piggly Wiggly Southern. They made the news by remaining one of only a few stores that did not open on Sundays and did not sell alcohol. In 1986, the announcement was made that the company was restructured as PWS Holdings after being purchased by Riordan, Freeman and Spogli, or RFS, an investment group out of Los Angeles, California. After forty-seven years, the little grocery company in Vidalia found itself again purchased by an investment group that planned to prop it up and sell it at a profit. But after the purchase, the offices and warehouse in Vidalia remained open. Company president Ronald Frost stepped down and became chairman of the board of directors. Lots of Piggly Wiggly employees left the company after the purchase and went to work at rival stores in South Georgia.

Rumors began to fly about the fate of Piggly Wiggly Southern two years later in 1988, when the names Bruno's and Food Lion were circulated as potential buyers. Food Lion was making moves in the state and building its own giant grocery warehouse in Jacksonville, Florida. Just a couple of days later, PWS Holdings was sold off when Bruno's finalized the deal, just a short time after RFS had unloaded another grocery chain it had purchased out west. As terms of the purchase, the warehouse and offices in Vidalia were closed permanently when PWS operations were moved to Bruno's corporate offices in Birmingham, Alabama. The Piggly Wiggly Southern stores were all then rebranded as Bruno's and FoodMax stores.

On December 13, 1975, Piggly Wiggly Southern was granted the trademarked name "Vidalia" to be used in marketing of its Vidalia onions. When the company moved from Vidalia to its new corporate headquarters in Birmingham, the Georgia Department of Agriculture was given the opportunity to own the certification mark, which was filed with the U.S. Patent and Trademark Office on February 2, 1990, and granted on August 18, 1992.

In 1990, the Vidalia Onion Committee organized the Vidalia Onion Hall of Fame. The Vidalia Onion Committee states this "award honors a person who has significantly and positively impacted the Vidalia onion industry." The very first inductee into the Hall of Fame that year was Gerald Achenbach.

7

A NEW VENTURE FOR
THE NEW BROTHERS

In 1972, a small produce buyer named Kenneth New talked his two sons, David and Danny, into going into business with him. The boys knew their father was onto something big in the produce business when he told them about his idea to market Vidalia onions. David left his job and Danny left college to get into the onion business and compete in an industry they knew nothing about. There weren't many onion producers at the time, and the onion business wasn't really going anywhere. New Brothers Inc. was formed and started marketing all the sweet onions they could buy. The onions they were selling were from the wrong county, Tattnall, and were usually labeled as "Glennville Sweets" or "Tattnall County Sweets." But when the onions were sold by the New Brothers, they would be called "Vidalia Sweets."

New Brothers did business in the Vidalia State Farmer's Market building on Stockyard Road, off U.S. Highway 280, on the eastern edge of town. In 1973, they turned over every rock and scraped up as many sweet onions as they could find and sold everything they could put their hands on. They drove as fast as they could to Collins one day when word came that a farmer had three acres of onions he was willing to sell. The pressures of the onion business took their toll on the oldest member of the team when Kenneth New died of a heart attack early in the season of 1974. He had been the experienced one and the one who came up with the ideas. The man died before the family had even settled on what they were gonna call this vegetable their father had talked them into dropping everything and chasing.

The brothers continued on without their father that year. They printed a custom onion bag with the name "VIDALIA GEORGIA" on it. The idea seemed like a good one to them, but they realized putting the city on a bag didn't pop like the name of what was inside, like putting Atlanta, Georgia, on a soda can instead of the name Coca-Cola. The buyers would call, and though they received a lot of grief from Tattnall County growers for their wording choice, still they marketed their onions under the name: Vidalia Onions.

Farmers around Toombs County still looked on onion farming as a losing game because of the struggles they had gone through in the 1940s, '50s and recent years. There were fewer than one hundred acres planted in the whole county in 1974 when the New Brothers rolled out their new "Vidalia Sweets." Phone calls were made and letters sent to promote a product that they didn't actually have their hands on. The company sold twenty-five thousand bags of Vidalia onions that winter. But in the end of the season, only five thousand bags were actually delivered. Every morning, the phone rang off the hook with produce companies looking for the rest of their onions. The Vidalia Sweets had sold like hotcakes, but there just weren't enough onions to fill the orders. That year, the New Brothers made their first out-of-state sale of Vidalia onions, even though it was to a store in Chattanooga.

In 1974, they realized they couldn't solely rely on Toombs County farmers for onions, and Tattnall County farmers gave them the stink eye for having the gall to label them Vidalia's. So the brothers decided to grow onions themselves. These men weren't farmers; they were produce salesmen. They didn't own a single acre of farmland or one piece of equipment. They rented land from friends and neighbors and hawked every equipment auction looking for something they could afford. After they'd purchased the bare minimum, they planted onions. Seedbeds were started, and when the transplants were big enough, they were plowed up and replanted in a field south of Santa Claus.

While the New Brothers waited for their onions to mature, they had to move their packing shed. The Georgia Department of Agriculture sold the state farmer's market they had been operating from to the City of Vidalia, where they built the Vidalia Recreation Department. The brothers moved across the road, constructed a shed with no walls or concrete floor and built a new operation to handle their crop. That 1975 crop turned out great and flew off the produce shelves. This "new" Vidalia onion was really just making a comeback. In 1976, they expanded to grow transplants for other farmers. That year, they grew 50 acres of transplants and 150 acres of onions.

The New Brothers were always looking to expand their business—and not just with fresh Vidalia onions. Since there wasn't a Vidalia onion on the grocery shelves for nearly three-quarters of the year, they decided to manufacture a line of canned food products containing Vidalia's they could sell the rest of the year. They first started chopping onions to produce New Bros. Vidalia Onion Relish. With their process fine-tuned, they expanded the line to include pickled onions, barbecue sauce, six flavors of salad dressings and Vidalia onion rings.

As the 1980s began, Vidalia onions were a hot commodity, which produced hot, as in *illegal*, illegitimate, substandard, non-Vidalia onions in a Vidalia onion bag, counterfeit onions. Enterprising individuals found they could drive to Texas or get a truck full of Texas onions delivered to Georgia and put them in a Vidalia onion bag they had somehow bought on the black market. These hot onions magically became Vidalia onions and were worth four or five times the price they should have brought. Unsuspecting customers, mostly northern travelers from Scranton or Sheboygan, wouldn't realize they'd been had til they got home. When the News found out even an empty Vidalia onion bag with their name on it fetched more than a full Texas onion bag, they knew they had to figure out how to thwart the onion pirates.

In those days, Vidalia onions only came in a sack. There were different-sized sacks but still an easy product to counterfeit. Untied, empty bags could be picked up at a grocery store or farmer's market or state-run farmers' market. The Texas onions came in fifty-pound bags and had "Yellow Onions" written on them. To transform them into Vidalia onions, all the pirates needed was a pocketknife and empty Vidalia onion bags. To confound the counterfeiters, the New Brothers bought a prepack machine that packed onions into smaller sealed mesh bags. Another first for the industry, compliments of the New Brothers. To further befuddle the reprobates, they bought a labeling machine that put a "New Bros Inc. A Certified True Vidalia Onion" sticker on every onion they produced, guaranteeing their authenticity. Neither of these technologies had ever been tried on a Georgia onion. The labeling machinery they wanted to use applied stickers to oranges, which were completely round with a slick, solid surface. Onions were different shapes and didn't always land in the right position for a sticker to be applied. Because they were shaped almost like a hockey puck, they'd flop when they needed to roll.

The New Brothers kept expanding their business and made sales further out into the country, which required advancements in processing and storage. They visited farms that handled other types of produce and applied these ideas to onions. After visiting a similar site out of state, at their processing facility, they built the first refrigerated onion storage rooms. Up until that time, everybody stacked bags under shelters and hoped to sell out before their stock rotted.

The New Brothers felt the need to go full steam ahead in 1984. Since they'd started, they hadn't been able to fulfill all the orders they received each year, fresh onions or onion products. The brothers hired an Atlanta advertising firm to promote their products in September 1983 with a budget exceeding $750,000. The company then investigated how to raise enough money to expand their business, for facility upgrades and farmland purchases. Eventually, they decided to sell stock in their company on NASDAQ. It wasn't easy; their first two underwriters went broke before their offering, so they had to underwrite the company themselves. After some hiccups, they went public, sold most of their stock and made most of the money they needed, but just not enough. After an initial public stock offering, or IPO, of one million shares at $5 per share, the shares didn't sell for what they needed to, and the quantity of shares didn't sell like they'd hoped.

Vidalia onions are a cold season crop, planted in the late fall, and sit in South Georgia fields through the winter. It's hard to kill an onion with cold weather or damage its quality. On Christmas Eve 1983, the temperature in the Vidalia area bottomed out at five degrees Fahrenheit. Onion farmers hadn't experienced those temperatures while handling that amount of onions being grown at that point, still only around one thousand acres. The onions appeared to have survived the cold and grew out of it. When the New Brothers began to pull their onions out of storage in the fall, they found that 20 percent of their crop had spoiled, a total value of $1 million. With the strain of knowing they had investors to satisfy, employees' retirement to maintain, and not just themselves and the local bank to make happy, somebody cooked the books to try to hide the losses. Employees traveled to Colorado to buy onion powder, create a paper trail to replace the rotten onions and make it look like nothing was missing. Fake accounts were opened at banks. A fake onion powder company was created out of thin air, but it had a real telephone number. One false step led to another until days seemed to be wasted covering their tracks. Danny broke under the strain of the deception, and the company called their lawyer and came clean about the whole thing. They handed over their new shed and equipment to their main local investor and managed to stay out of jail, but the New Brothers that restarted the Vidalia onion craze lost everything they'd worked for over a dozen hard years to build in a matter of days.

Danny New started feeling the early effects of multiple sclerosis when things were really beginning to take off during the 1980 season. He fought through the illness for several years. As you can imagine, the effects of MS severely cripple a person's ability to run a multimillion-dollar produce company. Still, he fought through the illness until the bitter end. In 2009, David and Danny New were inducted into the Vidalia Onion Hall of Fame.

8

PIRATES CLAIM A PIECE
OF THE ONION BOOTY

They say, "Imitation is the greatest form of flattery." Well, the Vidalia onion farmers weren't flattered at all when imitation Vidalia onions popped up in the market. No sooner had the market been established in 1977 when somebody started bootlegging the Vidalia onion. Although the culprit wasn't known, everybody knew they were shipping onions from Texas to Georgia and repackaging them in Vidalia onion bags. The reports were investigated by Georgia Department of Agriculture inspectors who turned up with nothing. Samples of Vidalia onions and onions from other states were sent to the GDA laboratory in Atlanta to see if there was a detectible difference. A Vidalia onion brought twice the price of a Texas onion, so there was plenty of incentive to play the stakes.

To combat the fraudulent onions, the Vidalia Chamber of Commerce printed up a tag to verify local onions were genuine. Although the effort had good intentions, some farmers didn't see it as being in their best interest. One of the biggest producers at the time, Danny New of New Brothers, complained, "These tags cost 15 cents each and it was going to cost us $240,000 for enough tags to mark our onions. The whole thing was nothing more than a fund-raising event for the chamber of commerce. None of the five oldest distributorships here belong to their program, and I'm hopeful this will be the only year of that."

In 1982, Tommy Irvin, Georgia's agriculture commissioner, personally received information that counterfeit Vidalia onions were being sold at the Atlanta State Farmers' Market in Forest Park. He traveled to the market and located about one thousand bags of ambiguous onions labeled as "The

Yumion onion tag distributed by the Vidalia Chamber of Commerce in 1983 to combat fraudulent onions. *Vidalia Onion Museum.*

Original World Famous Vidalia Onions." Required information for the label was missing, namely the grower and packer's names and addresses. The packer was soon identified as Seal Produce in Statesboro. The onions were guaranteed sweet by the "Sweet Onion Association." Since the onions were not properly labeled and there was no proof the "Sweet Onion Association" even existed, the Georgia Department of Agriculture embargoed the produce with a hearing in Atlanta set for the following Monday. Commissioner Irvin commented, "The onions I tasted were hot onions, much hotter than any Georgia sweet onion I ever ate. But they still claim they're Georgia onions." The onions were to be released for sale after they had been relabeled, presumably as anything but Vidalia onions.

When harvest time came in 1985, nothing had gone right since the onions had been planted. A freeze during planting season killed a huge chunk of the acreage and had to be replanted out of an estimated three thousand acres of onions that were grown that year. A cover story of the onion crop was featured in the *Market Bulletin*, noting the onions were marketed under several different names: Vidalia Sweet, Glennville Sweet, Georgia Sweet and Sweet Georgia. To combat imitation Vidalia onions, the Georgia legislature had just passed a bill dubbed the "Vidalia Onion Bill," strengthening the Georgia Food Act by increasing the possible fine of mislabeling a food from $1,000 per incident to $20,000. The Georgia Department of Agriculture also announced that it would be monitoring the Vidalia onion region and packing sheds more closely that season. Commissioner Irvin stated, "We hope problems with mislabeling will be minimal. We think that the strict penalty and the presence of agriculture employees will stop some of the problems we've experienced in the past with our onion crop."

The talk of imitation onions heated up early in the season when the price of sweet onions dropped by $6 a bag in just a couple of days. This caused a young farmer, Delbert Bland, who had invested a lot in the Vidalia onion business to go out and hire an investigator on his own dime. Bland described what happened:

> *So I got to checking around and looking into it. And looked for a private investigator. I knew Hugh Gillis from Swainsboro and found out his brother was a private investigator named Franklin Gillis. I paid him and he sat in the woods up there in Brooklet, Georgia, and took pictures of the folks working for Neilly pouring onions out of the back of a truck into a Vidalia bag. During the process, he took pictures of them, and they had guns on them. That's what was crazy. So anyway, no confrontation happened. When I got the pictures, I called Tommy [Irvin]. He said, "Alright, we'll go to court. 'Cause we've got to do something."*

The PI found where the onions were being bagged: a shed called Scott Farms as well as another facility in Morrow called Fairway Produce, both owned by a Georgia farmer named Raymond O'Neil Scott, also known as Neilly Scott. Fairway Produce was located west of the Southlake Mall in metro Atlanta. The origin of the yellow onions was determined to be Texas, California, Arizona and Wisconsin. When the onion imitator was located, the farmer hired workers to get hired on at the operation and report back to him with their findings. They witnessed in a short time the receiving, rebagging and relabeling of onions from other states as Vidalia onions right under the Vidalia onion farmers' noses. The operation was huge and rapidly expanding. There were tales of tractor trailers lining the highways from Texas to Georgia filled with yellow onions. All the shipper had to do was buy yellow onions for about $7 a bag, pay people to change their bags to pass them off as Vidalia onions and ship them out to stores and farmers' markets across the country for $25 a bag.

Bland contacted the Georgia Department of Agriculture and handed over his evidence. Sometime around April 19, other onion farmers contacted Jim Bridges, assistant commissioner with the department of agriculture, with concerns of out-of-state onions being brought into the area and rebagged as Vidalia onions. The farmers had two concerns: their prices had gone to nothing, and consumers were becoming confused. A meeting between four divisions of Georgia Department of Agriculture employees was held to discuss the problem. Within the week, every onion producer and handling facility was inspected by the task force. A district supervisor from GDA's Consumer Protection Division visited a farm named Scott Farms and was told by the owner he knew why he was there. It's not clear how far the supervisor got inside the operation because the commissioner of agriculture soon after called the Georgia Bureau of Investigation to assist with the investigation.

During this period, Assistant Commissioner Jim Bridges shared several phone calls with an onion seller and a lawyer associated with Scott Farms. Bridges told both of them there was no legal definition of a Vidalia onion, but the GDA considered it illegal to bring in onions from other states and sell them as Vidalia onions. Bridges then sent an inspector out to a facility called Fairway Produce in Morrow that was operated by Scott Farms and found it was operating without a packing license or surety bond.

On the night of May 14, two GBI agents set up a stakeout of the Scott Farms shed near Newington. Inside the shed were stacks of Texas onions in white and yellow bags next to fresh bags of Vidalia onions on pallets. The white and yellow Texas onion bags were immediately burned on the premises. The onions labeled as Vidalia onions were loaded onto a semitruck and left the shed at about 1:30 a.m. Nearing the end of the week, the GBI met with two individuals willing to go undercover at the shed to gather information. The two applied for work there and were hired.

On or around May 17, the GBI called to inform Assistant Commissioner Bridges that two confidential informants had been placed in the Scott Farms facility to observe its operations. The agent in charge asked him to have GDA personnel on standby to embargo the onions if the situation called for it. A Search and Seizure warrant was granted, allowing GBI and Screven County sheriff's agents to search the facility. Law enforcement agents questioned one of the confidential informants about his observations. He told the investigators they had been rebagging Everkrisp onions from Arizona as Vidalia onions and burning the empty bags. The new bags were labeled "Scott Farms Sweet Vidalia Onions Grown for & Distributed by Scott Farms, Brooklet, GA." After transferring, the bags were sealed with a tag, similar to the tags distributed by the Vidalia Chamber of Commerce, declaring they were "Certified Sweet Vidalia Onions."

The marketing director for the Georgia Department of Agriculture would later state, "There's too much incentive there. When you talk about a trailer load of onions with 800 bags on it, and that kind of difference in price, it's just too much temptation evidently for some of them to resist." Employees were unloading one trailer containing Arizona Everkrisp onions and loading another trailer with Vidalia onions. No onion grading was being done, with no culls or damaged onions reported with a large pile of empty Everkrisp bags observed on the shed floor. While there, two fully loaded tractor trailers of onions attempted to dock at the shed but were waved off by the shed's management. On the road near the facility, the onion trucks were stopped and inspected by the Screven County Sheriff's Office. The trucks were loaded with onions from Arizona with a destination of Scott Farms.

Late in the day, GDA personnel were contacted to withhold all onions in the Scott Farms packing shed to be withheld from commerce until they were released a week later. Before releasing the onions the next week, GDA contacted the Federal State Inspection Service to inspect the onions for damage or decay, to cover the department in case the onions had diminished while under embargo. The Federal State Inspection Service is a third-party auditor for agriculture commodities, including onions and peanuts, to ensure quality commodities are being traded. Its classifications and training are established by the USDA to meet or exceed the quality standards of their inspections. After the FSIS inspection, the onions were determined to be in the same state they had been in the week before.

The next week, the GBI found out about a third Scott Farms–operated shed near Interstate 95 in Ridgeland, South Carolina. The GBI met with Jasper County, South Carolina sheriff's deputies and the extension agent for the county. The warehouse was leased from the Jasper County Marketing Commission. At the shed were bags of onions labeled "Vidalia Sweet Onions" and yellow onions from five states other than Georgia, lots of empty bags, a couple of boxes of onion seals guaranteeing they were Vidalia onions and no grading equipment being used.

On May 29, a hearing was held and presided over by superior court judge Faye Martin of the Ogeechee Judicial Circuit at the courthouse in Millen. Depositions of GDA employees, GBI agents and produce executives were entered into the proceedings. The GBI's testimony of out-of-state onions coming into the shed and fetching three or four times the price after being rebranded as Vidalia onions was put into context. Testimony came from Joseph A. Cerniglia Jr., who was a produce dealer on the Atlanta market, executive chairman of the United Fresh Fruit and Vegetable Association and huge fan of Vidalia onions. He testified that Vidalia onions come from a certain region of Georgia that has special soil conditions. He stated that he expected to pay three to four times the price of other sweet onions and so did his customers. The same points were stated by the director of merchandising for the Kroger Company in Atlanta.

At the end of the hearing, the Georgia Department of Agriculture was granted a thirty-day restraining order against Scott Farms' owner Neilly Scott and his wife to immediately stop "misbranding their onions through the act and practice of rebagging out-of-state onions into bags labelled Vidalia sweet onions and selling them as Vidalia Onions" also "restrained and enjoined from selling or delivering, holding, storing, or offering for sale any out-of-state onions that have been rebagged into bags labelled Vidalia sweet or Vidalia onions." A follow-up hearing was set for June 18.

During the time the Scott Farms shed was under its temporary restraining order, Neilly Scott shipped out 9,339 sacks of rebagged "Vidalia onions" according to invoices turned over to the court. These were fifty-pound sacks, and at 800 bags per trailer load, Scott shipped out around a dozen whole truckloads of onions that he was instructed not to move or sell.

The GDA then handed down to the farmer a newly minted fine of $20,000 per violation. The fine had been only $1,000 the year prior, but the increase was signed by Governor Joe Frank Harris only a month before the violation was cited. Neilly Scott was playing with fire but never slowed down, cashing in a $14,000 profit per trailer load. With the restraining order granted, this gave the GDA about a month to figure out how to deal with the case. It also gave the Vidalia onion growers a little room to breathe. Plus, it also revealed that Neilly Scott may have found a crack in the rules that he was taking full advantage of. It's not clear whether he was the person who had been rebagging western onions on a large scale for the previous three years, but he had the process down and plenty of buyers. Neilly Scott was plowing full steam ahead until there was a legal definition of the Vidalia onion that proved what he was doing was illegal, of which so far there wasn't one.

In a written statement, the farmer's law counsel responded to the charges: "Scott Farms and Raymond O. Scott deny absolutely that they have violated any labeling law or any other law in the marketing of Vidalia onions. Scott Farms markets only true Vidalia onions under their labels. There is no scientific or other difference between the onions grown in Georgia and those grown in other parts of the South. Scott Farms grows true Vidalia onions in Georgia and also packs true Vidalia onions grown in other locations. These onions are identical in all respects and are true Vidalia's." A hearing was scheduled for June 18 at the Bulloch County Courthouse where the Department of Agriculture hoped to make the restraining order against rebagging onions permanent.

Tommy Irvin, Georgia's agriculture commissioner, said,

We have positive proof that onions grown in at least three other states have been rebagged into Scott Farms bags and are being marketed and sold as Vidalia onions, implying that they were produced in Georgia. We are very concerned that supermarkets and their customers around the country are buying a product with the belief that it was grown and produced in Georgia. Our producers of sweet Vidalia onions have worked long and hard at establishing a good reputation. Any tarnish to that reputation is a serious concern to me.

When word got around about the size of the rebagging operation, farmers speculated there could have already been more counterfeit Vidalia onions pass through the Scott shed than all the Vidalia onions grown in the whole state of Georgia by the time the raid occurred. Around May 20, Scott Farms had begun harvesting its own sweet onions grown in the Newington area. There were seventy-four acres of onions that the farm could have legally sold as Vidalias.

"In most cases the Texas onions are more pungent and hot to the taste, but the housewife in Atlanta can't go through the produce section and cut off a sample and taste it. That wouldn't be altogether too popular with the store management," stated a local county extension agent.

The Georgia Department of Agriculture law used to try to prohibit the counterfeiting of Vidalia onions was the Georgia Food Act. It is the law by which food safety and food labeling regulations for the state of Georgia are written. In 1985, there were requirements for the labeling of food containers that prohibited mislabeling. The GDA believed that was sufficient to say if an onion was from another state, no matter what its characteristics were, it couldn't be labeled as a Vidalia onion.

NEILLY SCOTT VERSUS ALL Y'ALL

When the court hearing date was finalized, Tommy Irvin stated that the farmer had been caught "red-handed": "The ruling for an evidentiary hearing is encouraging and we plan to proceed vigorously with the case. All evidence shows that Mr. Scott's sole intent was one of deception and fraud against consumers. His actions indicate that he knew what he was doing and that it was illegal." At a news conference set up by Neilly Scott's attorney, Scott told the crowd that the USDA assured him that "until the state of Georgia enacts legislation that can be enforced across the United States, any similar onion grown in the United States may be sold in interstate commerce as a Vidalia and not mislabeled."

Motions were entered by both sides of the case. The Georgia Department of Agriculture filed a motion to preempt the inclusion of chemical analysis comparisons of Vidalia onions and other yellow onions as well as the chemical composition of soils in the Vidalia district compared to other onion growing areas. The Scott Farms lawyers attempted to move some portions of the case to federal court because the onions hadn't been sold in Georgia. The motion to move from superior court to federal court was denied by U.S. District judge Dudley Bowen in Augusta on June 21.

A hearing of the Scott Farms case was held in superior court in Bulloch County to hear the merits of the case in late September 1985. The case was considered a civil case, No. 85-3205. When the two sides attended, the Department of Agriculture was represented by lawyers from the State Attorney General's Office under the direction of Attorney General Mike

Bowers. Neilly Scott had a new firm, Bouhan, Williams & Levy from Savannah, and a high-profile lawyer working on his case. Frank W. "Sonny" Seiler of Savannah is famous for bringing the first Uga bulldog to University of Georgia football games while he was a student there. He still owns Uga, while his son, Charles, takes care of the mascot during the week and delivers him to football games. Sonny Seiler was also representing another high-profile defendant around that time. A resident of Savannah, Jim Williams, had been charged with murder. His trial was immortalized by author John Berendt in the book *Midnight in the Garden of Good and Evil*.

The defense had decided to use the blatantly obvious as their defense: the loosely held definition, or lack thereof, of what a Vidalia onion was. In his opening offensive, Sonny Seiler criticized the Department of Agriculture for not addressing the problem, going back even further than Tommy Irvin's tenure, in office since 1969. "The guidelines should be there to steer you in the first instance, not after the fact. The commissioner of agriculture has got the cart before the horse. The commissioner could have enacted regulations that define Vidalia onions both by variety and production area and has failed. For 29 years, the department has ducked this responsibility."

The Agriculture Department decided to argue using common sense as its defense. Since they were called Vidalia onions, they had to come from Georgia, no matter what the law said. A state attorney representing the GDA stated, "You look to what housewives, restaurateurs and ordinary citizens think it is. Consumers know a Vidalia onion to be a Georgia-grown onion, not a Texas onion." Deputy Commissioner Jim Bridges admitted in his deposition that there wasn't an airtight definition of what a Vidalia onion was, but "the [state agriculture] department considers it illegal to sell onions grown in other states as Vidalia onions." Don Rogers, the marketing director for GDA, added: "The Agriculture Department's position has to be that a Vidalia onion, through the concept of people's minds, is one produced in Georgia, if not in a particular area. I don't know of another crop in Georgia that requires so much looking at. The peach has a little glamour, but it isn't so specialized as to make it a target."

The original judge in the case had stepped aside due to a previous encounter with the defendant as well as a recusal by all Ogeechee Judicial Court judges, so superior court judge Bryant Culpepper of the Macon circuit was assigned the case, and he clearly saw the daylight between the two sides.

You're telling me that someone in Rabun County can grow an onion, and it won't be of the same quality and Mr. Irvin is going to overlook that, whereas the same variety onion with similar properties grown in another state will be prohibited. You see the problem I have with that definition. This is controversy that's been going on for years without much resolution. Isn't it curious that the General Assembly, elected representatives, never could or would establish what a Vidalia onion is? There is no definition of a Vidalia onion, is there? Any onion grown in the city limits of Vidalia?

In response to the judge, the state attorney said, "We are just certain it is a Georgia-grown onion and it is known as such." The case would go to court on September 24, 1985. Judge Culpepper cleared his calendar to make room for the case, in anticipation that it would last about a week.

In documents released prior to the trial, a brochure used by Scott Farms to market their product was included. The front of the brochure stated "Hard to Believe! Scott Farms Inc. Announces The Original World-Famous Vidalia Sweet Onion. Certified by the Sweet Onion Association, Inc. Super Sweet's Vidalia Sweet Onions You Can Eat Like an Apple!" The back read "Scott Farms, Inc. Guarantees: Quality Onions And…Authentic World Famous Vidalia Sweet ONIONS. Look for this tag for your guarantee of a true Vidalia Sweet Onion." The tag pictured was similar to the ones used by the Toombs-Montgomery Vidalia Onion Growers Inc., reading, "The Original World Famous Vidalia Sweet Onion Quality Control. Certified Vidalia Sweet Onion Association, Inc. This is your guarantee of a TRUE VIDALIA SWEET ONION." The same wording had been used in the Seal Produce case in 1982. It was later revealed that Neilly Scott had also operated Seal Produce when the company was confronted about rebagged onions at the Atlanta State Farmers' Market a couple of years earlier. Along with eating, cooking and storage suggestions, there was a brief history of the Vidalia sweet onion:

This delicacy is grown in a small area of southeast Georgia, and is the only place this onion can be grown without becoming hot. Experts attribute this to the climate and soil texture of this small area and some even say the ozone layer there contributes to its sweet taste. Scott Farms, Inc. is located right in the heart of this onion country so you can be assured that every onion that comes from Scott Farms, Inc. is sweet and mild. Many have tried to duplicate its mildness, but none have been able to equal or surpass its unique taste. This is a seasonal onion and can only be purchased during the months of May and June, so be sure to stock up while they are fresh. If stored properly you can enjoy your delicious, sweet onions for many months.

This is a delicious vegetable that is taking the nation by storm, The SWEET ONION. No, not your ordinary onion, which brings tears to your eyes and unpleasant odor to your breath, but a delicious, mild, onion, known in its locale as the SUPER SWEET'S VIDALIA SWEET ONION. It is so sweet it is classified by some as a fruit and is often eaten like an apple. Scott Farms, Inc. of Brooklet, Georgia has been in the business of growing this sweet onion since 1975 and invites you to give them a try.

Tommy Irvin commented the Scott Farms brochure "verifies what we have contended from the inception what the general public perceives as a genuine Vidalia onion is grown in Georgia. When you're dealing in this area, and people are paying a premium for it, they expect something special for it. It's not just another onion." Scott Farms denied ever distributing the brochure but admitted that approximately one thousand copies had been stolen.

Without delay, the Great Onion Trial began in Statesboro on Tuesday morning, September 24, 1985. Many depositions from GBI agents, GDA employees, Scott Farms employees, and produce brokers were entered into the proceedings. According to records, on May 5, the first western onions of the season were rebagged into Vidalia onion bags at Scott Farms. That first shift rebagged five truckloads between the hours of 11:00 p.m. and 5:00 a.m. Working late at night for the next couple of weeks, workers rebagged twenty loads of onions. The operation was becoming so successful that the crew leader in charge of labor for both the shed and onion harvesting had to go to Texas to recruit more laborers. In his deposition, the crew leader stated he had been instructed by the owner to burn all the original onion bags and strings to prevent inspectors from finding them.

Gerald Goad's testimony provided some insight into what produce brokers were facing with these non-Vidalia "Vidalia onions." His company had purchased several truckloads of onions from Scott Farms labeled as "Vidalia onions" for eighteen dollars a bag. They were then offered as many loads as they wanted but ordered only five more. Goad then realized the onions he bought were not Vidalia onions but were from out west. He canceled the remainder of the order and stated that if he had wanted to purchase western onions to resell, he had sources to buy directly from. Another broker called Neilly Scott when he realized that he had received the wrong produce but was told not to worry. He told Scott that word had gotten around that his onions counterfeit but was personally guaranteed that all Scott onions were "genuine, Georgia-grown Vidalia onions."

Testimony revealed that a phone call was shared between Neilly Scott's attorney and the deputy commissioner of agriculture prior to the GBI raid. It was obvious from that news that Scott knew something big was about to go down. The deputy commissioner told him there was not a definition for Vidalia onions in the state law, but GDA considered rebagging Vidalia onions an illegal practice.

Late in the evening on Wednesday, the defense put its star witness on the stand. Paul Leeper was a horticulturist at Texas A&M who helped develop the Granex variety of onion that was being used to produce the Vidalia onion. Defense attorneys produced two bags of onions purchased that week that were both labeled "Vidalia." The scientist was asked to tell the two bags apart. He quickly determined that one bag of onions was spoiled. Since the trial was three or four months after the Vidalia onion harvest had ended, that was to be expected. The other onions were fresh but obviously from another state.

Leeper was then asked about the difference between Vidalia onions and other yellow onions. "The sweetness is controlled by genetics. Environment plays a very small part. That's why I said I couldn't tell any difference in a Granex onion from Texas or California or Georgia. They're all the same onion."

Sonny Seiler quipped, "A rose is a rose is a rose?"

"Certainly," was the reply.

As part of the agriculture department's case, Georgia State University conducted a survey of Georgia residents advertised in the *Market Bulletin*. Results indicated 95 percent of the respondents were aware of Vidalia onions, with about 75 percent believing that Vidalia onions should be grown only in Georgia.

On October 1, the judge released his written decision in what was a mixture of good news and bad news for both sides. Judge Culpepper's ruling stated: "The evidence presented in this case substantiates a finding that there is in the state a broad consumer perception that the 'Vidalia Onion' is at the very least, a Georgia grown product." The defendant's actions "tended to deceive because of the consumer perception that such onions are Georgia grown. Therefore, to take onions not grown in Georgia and rebag or resell them as 'Vidalia Onions' would be and is, a violation of the misbranding provisions of the Georgia Food Act." The judge again emphasized the need for a clear definition of what a Vidalia onion was in Georgia state law. "The growing, packing and distribution of Vidalia onions can at best be described as chaotic. If the commissioner fails to act, I think it's incumbent on the General Assembly to act. Rules and regulations giving guidance to the people in this industry are desperately needed."

Tommy Irvin's commented after the trial, "The judge has given us a definition, and it is precisely the definition we have used all along. His definition is explicit that an onion labelled as 'Vidalia' must be an onion produced in the state of Georgia, and rebagging out-of-state onions into bags labelled 'Vidalia' is a consumer fraud and deception." In a later comment, he stated, "After reviewing the judge's decision with the Attorney General, it is clear that the Department got everything it asked for, with the exception of a civil penalty. While I still believe a civil penalty is in order, we have decided that the time and expense involved in seeking an appeal would not be in the best interest of the state."

Vidalia Sweet Onion Market Survey that appeared in *Georgia Farmers and Consumers Market Bulletin*, August 1985. *Georgia Department of Agriculture.*

Deputy Commissioner Jim Bridges seemed pleased with the outcome: "I think it was victory. We were looking for a ruling that it was a violation of the Georgia Food Act and the judge so stated." The judge dropped the $20,000 fine from Scott Farms and instructed the Department of Agriculture to pay court costs.

Neilly Scott stated after the trial, "Thank God we had a judge with the sense to see through the things that's happened and rule for me and my family." In a foreshadowing of things to come, he also stated he would "never rebag another onion in the state of Georgia."

WRITING THE VIDALIA ONION ACT,
A COUPLE OF TIMES

As the Vidalia onion was starting to make its comeback, its acreage was tiny, but the price was huge. In 1980, there were fewer than three hundred acres of sweet onions grown in Georgia. Toombs and Montgomery Counties produced about half of the onions grown. There were eighty acres of onions grown within the Vidalia city limits, by David and Danny New. Word got out that there was an enterprising individual buying onions from out of state and putting them in a "Sweet Vidalia bag." In two weeks, he had profited $10,000. In response, growers pulled together and created associations to combat outside forces from destroying the market: the Vidalia Onion Growers and Distributors Association, the Toombs County Vidalia Onion Growers Association and then later the Toombs-Montgomery Vidalia Onion Growers Inc. Tags from the Vidalia Chamber of Commerce Onion Commission featured the new Vidalia Onion Ambassador, Yumion. Tags and seals were sold to growers to add proof that customers were buying the real thing. The associations first used tags, which were quickly pirated. Then they went to numbered seals and tags, with each farmer receiving specific tags that could be traced if they were copied or misused. Each year's tag was different to throw off the counterfeiters, who then started selling in places where people had heard of Vidalia onions but just weren't aware of the tags.

The local county extension agent laid out the situation:

> *If all of the growers could get together and agree on a label, then this area would really experience some growth in its onion crop. You know this onion*

*is a temperamental crop. Almost as temperamental as the growers. It seems
a shame that right here we have this tremendous gift, where a Texas Granex
onion changes into a sweet onion. We don't know why or how. But it's our
gift and we are not taking full advantage of it because of bickering, brother
against brother, neighbor against neighbor.*

Talking about the onion industry in the area, the county extension director
said, "The little feller is not realizing its full potential. Maybe the income
from the Vidalia onion here in Toombs is a quarter of a million dollars a
year. I don't really know. You can't get a handle on it because onions aren't
a controlled crop, and no grower is going to advertise what he's growing
or getting. That's one of the problems; we have got to work together." The
Tattnall County Extension director said, "Generally, we had about 275
acres in onions last year with about 375 bags per acre that's a 50-pound bag.
And, generally, getting about $12 per bag you can figure it out at about $1.2
million, somewhere in there."

By 1983, the Vidalia Chamber of Commerce's Vidalia Sweet Onion
Commission's tag program had grown tremendously. There were now
fifty growers participating, producing over one thousand acres of Vidalia
onions in the three-county area. That year, 230,000 Vidalia onion tags were
expected to be distributed. Jack Walden, the executive vice president of the
chamber, said, "Since the 1980 season, we have invested almost $100,000 in
advertising and promotion of our world-famous product. The 1983 effort will
be as important as any we have yet undertaken." Also, a big advancement in
the industry that addressed uniform quality was the institution of a grading
program. The farmers requested a USDA inspection for the crop where only
onions receiving a #1 quality grade could be classified as a Vidalia onion.

That year in Atlanta, a bill was proposed in the Georgia legislature
attempting to define the Vidalia onion. The easy part was defining what it was:
a yellow onion grown in Georgia. The hard part was defining where it could
be grown. The farmers in Toombs, Montgomery and Treutlen Counties
had worked together for a number of years trying to establish the Vidalia
onion. The first bill introduced by Clinton Oliver, a state representative
from Glennville, defined a small Vidalia onion area that contained Treutlen,
Montgomery, Toombs, Tattnall, Long and Evans Counties. Representative
John Godbee from Bulloch County submitted a similar bill that added
Emanuel, Candler and Bulloch Counties. Pete Phillips, representative from
Soperton, wanted Wheeler County added. Representative Bobby Lane
from Statesboro stated he wanted Screven County added. While asking the

lawmakers to allow him to continue to grow the onions, W.J. Grimes from Wheeler County cleared up the confusion as to where the boundaries should be: "Nobody knows where you can grow this onion and where you can't. Anywhere you can grow a long-leaf pine, you can grow Vidalia onions."

The next move was across the hall, by Senator Hugh Gillis from Soperton. He introduced a bill defining the "Vidalia Production Area" as Toombs, Tattnall, Montgomery, Wheeler, Emanuel, Candler and Bulloch, with portions of Dodge, Laurens, Treutlen, Evans, Appling, Wayne, Long, Telfair and Jeff Davis. This inclusive area was opposed by the farmers and city officials of the Vidalia area, some of the same folks who proposed the bill. Dick Walden of the Toombs-Vidalia Chamber of Commerce said, "We are going to do everything we possibly can to see there is no bill passed. Everyone has been offered such extreme amendments, that, at the present time, we feel no bill would be better than this."

After the court case against Scott Farms, everybody put aside their differences and worked to produce a bill for the governor to sign prior to the 1986 season. Everybody knew they would be replaying last year's events if a definition of a "Vidalia onion" wasn't spelled out in state law beforehand. Senator Bill English from Swainsboro told the press, "If we don't put in place a law within this marketing season, you can stand back and let the trucks from Texas, Florida and other places and let those onions go out with Vidalia labels."

A hearing was held in the legislature on January 7 by the agriculture commissioner to propose the Vidalia Onion Act. The production area that was scrapped in 1983 was reintroduced. After the hearing, the bill was changed by adding in all of Bacon County, southern Screven County and an eastern section of Dodge County into the Vidalia Onion Production Area. But there were still a dozen farmers who were about to be left out in the cold because they didn't farm inside the described "Vidalia Onion Production Area." In order to allow them to continue producing Vidalia onions without making the production area be the entire state, a compromise was reached. According to the Vidalia Onion Law of 1986: "The Commissioner is authorized to grant variances in the production area requirements of this article to any producer who has produced in Georgia, marketed, and labeled onions of the Vidalia onion variety as Vidalia onions prior to January 31, 1986." Folks had to prove they had grown Vidalia onions in the past, mostly using receipts for seedlings, seeds or from sales of their onions. Farmers that proved they were growing onions prior to that date included a farmer all the way down in Seminole County; two in metro Atlanta in Douglas and Gwinnett Counties; and

Map of Georgia's Vidalia Onion Production Area as designated in the Vidalia Onion Act of 1986. *Author's collection.*

farmers in Laurens, Coffee, Tift, Berrien, Dooly, Taylor, Washington, Worth and Irwin. Even Emmett Reynolds, the mayor of Arabi, who once served as Georgia's state Farm Bureau president, grew Vidalia onions.

The Vidalia Onion Act of 1986 was introduced by Bob Lane of Statesboro on Monday, January 13. It was approved by the House Agriculture Committee by a vote of 17–2 on Wednesday, the fifteenth, and sent to the House floor, where it quickly passed by a vote of 153–8 on Friday, the seventeenth. Among the dissenters were Newt Hudson of Rochelle, Earleen Sizemore of Sylvester and Sonny Watson of Warner Robins. The act was approved by the senate with a vote of 52–0 on January 31. The bill was immediately signed by Governor Joe Frank Harris since Tommy Irvin had asked the legislature to speed the bill through as quickly as possible so it could be enacted for the 1986 Vidalia onion crop.

Tommy Irvin released a statement, saying,

> *I am gratified that the legislature saw fit to give us the teeth to adequately enforce truthful labelling of Vidalia onions. Through the rules and*

regulations we have already drawn up, and by true limiting production to the heart of historical Vidalia onion production, I believe we have ensured a growing and viable market for this premium, and profitable Georgia product, whose reputation was being tarnished by unscrupulous refused to levy penalties against operators.

According to the Vidalia Onion Act of 1986:

Only onions which are of the Vidalia onion variety and which are grown within the Vidalia onion production area may be identified, classified, packaged, labeled, or otherwise designated for sale inside or outside this state as Vidalia onions. The term "Vidalia" may be used in connection with the labeling, packaging, classifying, or identifying of onions for sale inside or outside this state only if the onions are of the Vidalia onion variety and are grown in the Vidalia onion production area.

The rest of the act fills in the blanks left by the previous passage. To be able to adjust to conditions and the changing of the times, the act authorized the agriculture commissioner to "prescribe rules or regulations which may include, but not necessarily be limited to, quality standards, grades, packing, handling, labeling, and marketing practices for the marketing of onions in this state, including the requirements that all Vidalia onions be initially packed only in the Vidalia onion production area." The selection process for varieties of onion seed used to grow Vidalia onions was spelled out in the act. Vidalia onions are grown from "Allium Cepa of the hybrid yellow granex, granex parentage, or other similar varieties." The University of Georgia would evaluate new varieties and make recommendations.

To address the counterfeit Vidalia onion market, a section was written specifically for that purpose:

It shall be unlawful for any person to sell or offer for sale either inside or outside this state any onions as Vidalia onions unless such onions are of the Vidalia onion variety and were grown in the Vidalia onion production area. (b) It shall be unlawful for any person to package, label, identify, or classify any onions for sale inside or outside this state as Vidalia onions or to use the term "Vidalia" in connection with the labeling, packaging, classifying, or identifying of onions for sale inside or outside this state unless such onions are of the Vidalia onion variety and were grown in the Vidalia onion production area. Any person who violates subsection (a) or (b) of this

Code section shall be guilty of a felony and, upon conviction thereof, shall be punished by a fine of not less than $1,000.00 nor more than $5,000.00 or by imprisonment for not less than one nor more than three years, or both.

The Vidalia Onion Advisory Panel was also created by the Vidalia Onion Act: "The Commissioner shall appoint a Vidalia Onion Advisory Panel, to consist of individuals involved in growing, packing, or growing and packing Vidalia onions; at least one county cooperative extension agent from the Vidalia onion production area; and any other person or persons selected by the Commissioner, for the purpose of rendering advice upon his or her request regarding the exercise of his or her authority."

By law, the commissioner held a hearing at the agriculture building across from the capitol on March 4 for comments to be filed. Without any major changes or opposition, the rule was filed with the Georgia Secretary of State's Office on March 11. Three weeks later on April 1, 1986, the Vidalia Onion Act of 1986 became law.

In the Vidalia Onion Act, there are provisions for the collection of fees on food products that carry the Vidalia onion name that contain some of the onions as ingredients and grades and standards for grading onions by the USDA. In 2005, a provision to create a shipping date for onions was added to the Vidalia Onion Act.

THE VIDALIA ONION GROWS UP

I n 1987, the next logical step for the Vidalia onion farmers was to form a commodity commission. Agricultural commodity commissions are typically devoted to promotion, education and research of the given crop, also referred to as a commodity. To function, money has to be collected from the sale of the crop at a small price per selling unit: by the bushel, pound or head. In order to form a Vidalia Onion Commodity Commission, ten growers were nominated and then five would be approved by Georgia agriculture commissioner Tommy Irvin and Georgia Farm Bureau president Bob Nash, with one ex-officio member each appointed by the Georgia House of Representatives and Senate. After their appointment to the commission panel, they would then work with the Department of Agriculture and Farm Bureau to navigate the process of forming a marketing order to create the commission. The commission officers were then charged with formulating a ballot for growers to vote on and then distribute ballots to all eligible voters.

At least 51 percent of the onion farmers had to vote, and 51 percent of the votes cast by the registered onion growers had to be in support of the commodity commission for it to pass. For the vote to count, the voters who approved the commission had to produce 51 percent of the Vidalia onion crop. The commission would be funded at a proposed rate of $0.07 per fifty-pound bag, which was sold for about $15.00 at that time, a rate of .5 percent. The commission panel was approved with Irvin and Nash serving as ex-officio members. Two educational hearing were held, one at the Tattnall County Courthouse and one at the Toombs County Courthouse. After a unanimous vote by the panel, the referendum was presented to the growers for approval. Ballots were then distributed on April 22, with a return deadline of May 21. When asked about the need for a commodity commission for onions, the Department of Agriculture's director of commodities promotion, Richey Seaton, said, "Vidalia onion farmers have created a specialty market. Now comes the hard part: they've got to fight to keep it. Texas is miles ahead of us in terms of marketing and promotion. That's the thing that concerns me. Are we going to sit back and take what the market gives us, or get out there and pitch for a part of it?"

After the votes were counted at the Toombs County Courthouse on May 26, the referendum failed to be passed. There were 130 votes cast out of 240 ballots sent. Out of the 130, 78 voted yes. Some of the farmers sat out of the voting because they didn't want to be charged seven cents per bag while some were mad that they didn't have a chance to nominate a grower of their choice to be eligible for the commodity panel. Either way, the voting turned south, so the panel members turned their attention north toward Washington, D.C. Their only hope to organize would be a federal marketing order to protect the Vidalia onion.

A group was formed to create a USDA-mandated federal marketing order in the summer of 1988. The group was called FAVOR, or Farmers Allied for a Vidalia Onion Referendum, and chaired by W.J. Grimes of Wheeler County. A two-day hearing was held on the issue at the Toombs County Courthouse in September 1988. The hearing was administrated by the USDA and overseen by an administrative law judge. W.J. Grimes organized the nearly two dozen witnesses giving testimony to support a federal marketing order, including farmers, shippers, researchers from the University of Georgia and U.S. Representative Lindsey Thomas. When he took the stand, Grimes speculated that 40 percent of the Vidalia onions sold in the United States were fake. He told the judge, "Persons in other areas are engaging in deceptive and misleading trade practices by selling other onions under the Vidalia name. This causes confusion, dissatisfaction and rejection among consumers, and severe economic damage to producers and handlers."

After the failed vote for a state marketing order, the climb would be steeper in the federal marketing order vote. Two-thirds of the growers, or at least growers who produced two-thirds of the crop, would have to approve the order. Then it would have to be approved by the USDA secretary. The proposed marketing order was formulated by the farmers and delivered to the USDA for inspection. Delbert Bland described the trip to Washington:

The federal marketing order was a whole other story. When we got the state law, that was great, as long as you were in the state. But when you're not in the state, they've got to honor the state's rules, but they don't have to abide by them. So five of us went to Washington DC: me, R.T. (Stanley), R.E. (Hendrix), Bob Cato and W.J. (Grimes). We went to Wyche Fowler's office. On the way up there, I called Sam Nunn and talked to his secretary. She said there wasn't hardly no way he could come to a meeting today. He was booked head over heels. I told her what we were doing, who I was, all that there. We sat down in Wyche Fowler's office, at the time Reagan was in office. The Secretary of Agriculture started telling us that there wasn't no way we were going to get a federal marketing order that this administration wasn't that keen on and this was going to take time. All of a sudden, Sam Nunn walked in the room. They had him a seat right by me. He sat and didn't say a word. And that guy (Secretary of Agriculture) went from no marketing order to being as nervous as a housecat in a room full of rocking chairs trying to write that marketing order and how quick he could get it wrote. And that's the first time I ever witnessed what power and politics will do. It blew my mind. We got our marketing order and got home that same day, boss!

After the USDA approved the marketing order, there would have to be a hearing for comments. The comments would then have to be evaluated and addressed. If the referendum passed through the process, it would be distributed to the growers for a vote.

The marketing order vote was aided by news of a familiar name, and fellow Georgia farmer, who moved his onion packing business out of state, to Muleshoe, Texas, on the Texas–New Mexico border. Located between Lubbock and Clovis, New Mexico, Kent Scott was selling Vidalia onions that weren't grown in the newly designated "Vidalia Onion Production Area" but somewhere in Texas or New Mexico. The produce was marketed as a "Sweet Vidalia Onion" that was grown from the same variety as the Vidalia onions but over one thousand miles to the west. The onions didn't grow along the Ohoopee River but near the Double Mountain Forks of the Brazos River. Using the same argument from the court case in 1985, the farmer believed genetics, not geography made the onions sweet.

When interviewed by phone, the farmer answered, "Yes, I ship a Vidalia, but it's not Georgia-grown. I am shipping a true Vidalia, a Y-33 hybrid granex onion. It's not the soil or climate, but the genetics that make it a sweeter onion. Just like you and I are products of the genetics of our mother and father." The farmer spoke to reporters from his office in Brooklet, Georgia, and was the brother of the man found to be rebagging western state onions as Vidalia onions in Newington, Georgia. The operation was locked in a legal battle with the Georgia Department of Agriculture in 1985 for doing the exact same thing but inside the boundaries of the state of Georgia. Just like the speed limit in Georgia didn't matter in Texas, neither did the Vidalia Onion Act of 1986.

"We're not getting into the argument of which is best. It's just that when you buy a Vidalia onion, you wouldn't feel comfortable if it was coming from Texas. The consumer…expects a Vidalia onion to come from east of the Mississippi River. The consumers are getting ripped off," said W.J. Grimes. "If it were a cheaper onion, nobody would fake it. But the Vidalia is a special onion. It's not just a sweet onion, it's a Vidalia onion. It's something that has made its own reputation over the past 40 to 50 years, slow and gradual. It takes a good product to do that without any promotion money. People want a Vidalia onion, and that many people can't be wrong."

In March 1989, the USDA held a referendum at the Toombs County Courthouse for onion producers to vote, but not for thirty days like with the failed state marketing order vote the year before but for only three. Out of about 250 registered growers, 147 came to the courthouse to participate. The 51 percent threshold was in place for the referendum and was cleared by about 20 voters. The marketing order was passed by over 98 percent of the vote. "I'd bet you my hat that we won't get a half a dozen negative votes, and my hat is real important to me," said W.J. Grimes. The hat he referenced was his white cowboy hat he wore everywhere. It was his trademark. The only photo of him found without his hat on was taken in the office of Senator Wyche Fowler on Capitol Hill. After the vote was counted, there were only 3 negative votes cast against the order. After the vote was made public, Grimes said, "This just proves what can be done when everybody's pushing in the same direction at the same time."

The USDA Marketing Order 955 mirrored the Vidalia Onion Act of 1986's definition of a Vidalia onion and the Vidalia Onion Production Area. The only difference was, this order carried weight throughout the entire country and not just Georgia like the Onion Act.

The marketing order defined the Vidalia Onion Committee, its membership, term length and their duties. The committee is made up of nine members, eight producers and one "public member." The public member is considered a stakeholder with an outside perspective on the business of the committee. The Vidalia Onion Committee is different from the Vidalia Onion Advisory Panel, but the members may be the same

Left: Robert Grist, Tommy Irvin, New York City mayor Ed Koch, W.J. Grimes and two grocery executives pay a visit to the mayor's office. *Jimmy Grimes.*

Below: Vidalia onion growers, including Delbert Bland and W.J. Grimes, and executives meet with U.S. Senator Wyche Fowler, in his Washington, D.C. office. *Jimmy Grimes.*

people. Duties of the committee include administering marketing order, making rules and regulations to carry out the marketing order, collecting and reporting to the USDA compliance issues and recommending amendments to the USDA secretary.

In the mid-1990s, a couple of South Georgia farmers attempted to have their onions added to the marketing order so they also could grow Vidalia onions. The onions were sold as Tift Sweets and Ty Ty Sweets, but that was as far as anybody was willing to go. "When the word Vidalia is mentioned, it kind of ruffles your feathers. I can grow onions as good as anyone in this state," said Buddy Talley of his Tift Sweets. "Ty Ty's don't move as well as Vidalia, even though they are the same variety," said Jim Parrish, who grew Ty Ty Sweets. The Georgia House of Representatives agriculture committee held two hearings in the summer of 1993, one in Tifton and one the next day in Lyons. Agriculture Commissioner Tommy Irvin answered the question: "If Mr. Parrish wants to grow Vidalia's, he can buy a farm in the region and grow and sell all he wants. Everybody can't grow onions and market them as Vidalia's." The Vidalia Onion Production Area has remained unchanged since the laws were written. When the Vidalia Onion Act of 1986 was signed, there were twelve farmers granted variances that allowed them to grow Vidalia onions outside the growing area. One of those farmers was allowed to grow Vidalia onions in Tift County.

During the 1990 legislative session of the Georgia Assembly, Representative Fisher Barfoot introduced a bill to designate the Vidalia Sweet Onion as the Georgia State Vegetable. Barfoot was a representative in his first term for Toombs, Montgomery, Treutlen and Wheeler Counties. In 1988, he replaced Pete Phillips's widow, who was filling her husband's seat after he died in office. Barfoot started working at the Dublin Piggly Wiggly in high school and was promoted a store manager position when he was only eighteen. He served as president of the Georgia Agribusiness Council for several years and as vice president of marketing for the Piggly Wiggly Southern Company before retiring in 1988.

House Bill 1572 was debated in the House Agriculture and Consumer Affairs Committee with one representative suggesting the collard green be named the state vegetable instead. After he said his peace, the committee approved the bill and sent it to the full House for a vote. When it passed with a vote of 164 to 0, not even the representative in favor of collard greens had the heart to vote against it. After approval by a vote of 43 to 0 in the Senate, the president of the Senate, Zell Miller, approved the bill on a desk full of Vidalia onions. Finally, Governor Joe Frank Harris signed the bill into law on April 11, 1990.

Two weeks after the Vidalia onion became the Official State Vegetable, on April 25, 1990, a historic marker for Vidalia onions was unveiled and later placed in front of the Walmart on Highway 280 near the Mose Coleman farm, the first place where Vidalia onions were grown. The dedication was held during the Vidalia Sweet Onion Festival at Vidalia City Hall and

Historic marker designating Mose Coleman's farm where Vidalia onions were grown. *Author's collection.*

attended by the Coleman family. During the ceremony, local historian Bill Warthen spoke about the history of the Vidalia onion. The marker read:

> ### HOME OF THE VIDALIA SWEET ONION
> *One of the first crops of Vidalia Onions was commercially grown near this site in 1931 by Moses Coleman, a local farmer. The onion is planted in a 20-county area from September through February and is harvested from late April through early June. Vidalia Onions are very low in pungency due to a combination of the native soils being low in sulfur and growing in a mild climate. The onions, grown in this 20-county area, have developed an international reputation as the "world's sweetest onions." The Vidalia Onion was named Georgia's official vegetable in 1990 and is a major state industry.*

HOW MR. GRIMES AND DR. SMITTLE
CHANGED THE INDUSTRY

I n 1921, the University of Georgia opened the Coastal Plains Experiment Station in Tifton, Georgia. Dr. O.J. Woodard was one of the first researchers to begin work there. His first test crop was sweet potatoes. The CPES evolved and expanded, and in the 1970s, a research scientist named Dr. Doyle Smittle was working there. His earliest mentioned work was on the effects of irrigation frequency in vegetables.

In 1979, Dr. Smittle conducted a taste and chemical analysis of onions from six Georgia counties and from Texas. Nine judges were selected for a taste test of the onions. Laboratory equipment was used to test nitrogen, sugar, sulfur and pungency. Onions from Berrien, Colquitt, Tift, Wheeler, Toombs and Tattnall Counties were tested. After the test results were known, Dr. Smittle stated: "Realistically, I'd have to say there is no difference in Georgia onions from those counties tested. There was a preference for all the Georgia onions over those from Texas, however." He found that taste preference was linked to the amount of pungency in the onion, which depends on the amount of sulfur in it. "How the onions are grown is more important than where they are grown as long as it's in sandy soil. The difference in one grower to another in a county is more of a factor than the difference between counties." He explained why results for the onions in Georgia were so similar: "Soils below the Fall Line aren't that different, but I could see the Vidalia name restricted to the Granex grown in sandy soil below the Fall Line. But I don't want to get into second guessing what limits are placed on the name 'Vidalia onion.' I am only concerned with the scientific aspects, not the political ones."

In 1978, Dr. Smittle met with a Wheeler County onion farmer named W.J. Grimes, locally known as Junior Grimes. Grimes farmed in an area where Telfair, Dodge, Wheeler and Laurens Counties all met and farmed in all of them at one time or another. He had grown produce for many years and was approached in the early 1970s about trying to grow something called Vidalia onions for Piggly Wiggly by their produce buyer, Frank Fountain. Grimes and his son Jimmy farmed in the sandy soil region north of the Little Ocmulgee State Park and along Highway 441.

W.J. Grimes inspects his onion crop in his Wheeler County field in the mid-1990s. *Jimmy Grimes.*

During their time growing onions, the Grimes family grew about nine hundred acres of mostly the Granex 33 onion variety. In talking to Dr. Smittle, Grimes told him about the problem onion farmers had. At the time, farmers stored their onions under shelters in mesh bags and hoped they didn't rot before they were sold. Oftentimes, if the onions didn't rot on the farm, they'd rot on the grocery store shelves or at a customer's home. All a farmer could hope for was to sell all his onions in a little over a month's time. Unless their onions' shelf life could be extended, there was no reason to grow more onions. W.J. Grimes believed that he could sell more onions if he could expand his window of opportunity.

Dr. Smittle went back to the CPES in Tifton to come up with a plan. He studied changes to the planting dates of onions, which varieties held up best in storage and what effect cold storage had on onions. After trial and error, changes to the first two variables proved unprofitable. There was only one remaining option, so in 1983, Dr. Smittle settled on cold storage as the only way to lengthen the season.

The state of Michigan is a huge apple producer and developed a storage technique around World War II that extended the shelf life of apples dramatically. The technique is called Controlled Atmospheric Cold Storage. Several factors in the refrigerated environment are adjusted to prevent apples from rotting or just plain disintegrating over time. Dr. Smittle borrowed some Grimes onions and headed back to Tifton to begin the process of finding

Above: W.J. and Jimmy Grimes stand in front of fifty-pound Vidalia onion boxes ready to ship at their farm. *Jimmy Grimes.*

Left: Jimmy and W.J. Grimes pose in their onion field outside Helena. *Jimmy Grimes.*

how to store onions for six months. He didn't have the resources to build an entire storage facility of any size, so he drilled holes in three five-gallon buckets and ran tubing into them. There he could change the environment one factor at a time to find the right combination. He experimented with concentration levels of oxygen, nitrogen, carbon dioxide, temperature and humidity. In 1984, he felt that his experiment was a success. He told the

Top: Grimes Farms Onion bags and boxes. *Jimmy Grimes.*

Middle: Grimes Farms Onion bags. *Jimmy Grimes.*

Bottom: Pallets of fifty-pound boxes of Grimes Farms onions ready to ship. *Jimmy Grimes.*

media, "If we can store an apple for nine months, we should be able to store an onion you can eat like an apple for nine months." In speaking about the experiment's results, he said, "The onions worked beautifully last year. We were able to have good quality onions until after Thanksgiving. The ones we didn't store under special conditions, controlled atmosphere conditions, we didn't have any left at that time of year." In 1986, Smittle kept onions sealed in his white buckets from May until Thanksgiving. He opened the containers and taste-tested them with the farmer he got the onions from, Grimes. When they tasted the six-month-old onions, Grimes started pushing Dr. Smittle to finish the job because he knew he had found the answer to the storage problem. He then increased the test batch to two hundred pounds in a CA storage room and two hundred pounds in a regular refrigerated room with no modified atmosphere for thirty-two weeks. At the end of the test, 83 percent of the CA storage onions were edible compared to 28 percent of the refrigerated onions. At the end of the test, Dr. Smittle told the media, "This will change the Vidalia onion industry."

Dr. Smittle and Grimes took a trip in 1989 to meet with researchers from Michigan State University, where they toured an apple CA storage facility and hoped to replicate the technology and adapt it to onions. When Dr. Smittle was confident in his results, it was time to go full-scale with the CA experiment. Grimes said, "With the bumper crop of 1988, when we couldn't give them away, twenty thousand bags were sent to Michigan for a CA experiment." Twenty thousand fifty-pound bags added up to one million pounds of onions. The onions were pulled at six weeks—they were wet and had sprouted. The differences between onions and apples were plenty, affecting the results of the experiment. Apples are fruit from a tree while onions are the base of a plant's stalk that also contains part of the root. A tiny amount of moisture triggers regeneration, or regrowth of the plant from either the roots or the stem. An apple cannot regenerate because it lacks "stem cells" that can produce growth from either end of the onion.

The CA storage room in Michigan proved that humidity was an important factor that had to be handled differently than with apples. With the right equipment and Grimes willing to take the next big step, plans to build a special warehouse in the middle of nowhere were made. Electrical lines had to be added to the area to feed the mechanical refrigeration and atmosphere modification equipment. Construction began in October 1988 on the first CA storage facility for Vidalia onions on a two-lane county road between Alamo and Helena. Construction was conducted in the winter, and a sixty-thousand-bag-capacity cooler was finished in time to load onions from the

Dr. Doyle Smittle in his lab at the University of Georgia–Tifton Campus with buckets of onions as part of his Controlled Atmospheric Storage experiment. *University of Georgia-Tifton.*

1989 crop inside. The room was loaded with about seven thousand fifty-pound bags—not quite quarter capacity—of fresh Vidalia onions at the end of May and sealed till the fall. Invitations went out to every onion farmer in the state, all 250 of them. Lots of them and the Georgia commissioner of agriculture, Tommy Irvin, showed up to see the opening of basically a time capsule from May 1989. On November 2, 1989, Tommy Irvin cut the ribbon on the CA. The door was opened, and samples were given out to test. The onions tasted sweet and had the right texture, just like they did when they were put in storage. After the taste-testing was over, the remainder of onions was shipped to Publix Supermarkets in Florida. Greg Sciullo, produce director for Publix, later said, "We didn't really know what to expect as to overall quality. The experiment, from Mr. Grimes's end and the one on our end was extremely successful. We anticipated selling the Vidalia's during Thanksgiving and Christmas, but the entire load was gone in less than five days, selling at ninety-nine cents a pound."

Arnold Horton from Little Ocmulgee EMC explained the CA process: "The air we breathe is 21 percent oxygen, 78 percent nitrogen and a small amount of carbon dioxide. For onions, we lower the oxygen to 3 percent, increase the nitrogen to 92 percent and carbon dioxide to 5 percent. The

Left: Controlled Atmospheric Storage grand opening press conference at Grimes Farms. Publix executives at podium. *Jimmy Grimes.*

Right: Ribbon cutting at Grimes Farms Controlled Atmospheric Storage. Pictured are W.J. Grimes, Tommy Irvin, W.J. Grimes family. *Jimmy Grimes.*

controlled atmosphere is a modification of the chemical elements that already exist in the air we breathe." Cold temperatures prevent regrowth and decay from bacteria. Low oxygen prevents root growth and prevent sugar loss. Increased carbon dioxide prevents an increase in pungency.

During the ribbon-cutting ceremony, a ten-pound box of Grimes Farms Vidalia onions was taken from the CA room to be auctioned off. The onions brought $1,300 from the highest bidder. The money raised was donated to continue Dr. Smittle's research on Vidalia onions. He admitted that the results at Grimes Farms was better than expected, but still much was needed to be done. "The apple industry is still working on CA research after forty-five years of use. Forty years from now, I'll still be fine-tuning," said W.J. Grimes.

Everybody was impressed and started working on getting their own CAs. The electrical grid had to be beefed up in the areas where CAs were planned. One thing that worked in the growers' favor was the Georgia Power nuclear powerplant sitting right across the river in Appling County, producing more than enough electricity for the region. The Georgia Development Authority helped with low-interest loans to make the projects happen. The

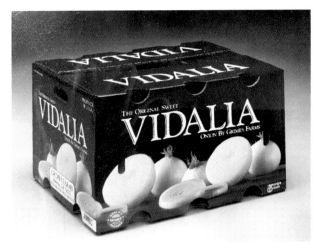

Left: Grimes Farms fifty-pound Vidalia onion box. *Jimmy Grimes*.

Below: Controlled Atmospheric Storage installation at Grimes Farms. *Andy Stanton*.

first full-sized Controlled Atmosphere Storage Facility was opened in August of the very next year. W.J. and his son Jimmy Grimes also went all in on the installation of CAs on their farm, adding a dozen CA rooms to their facilities outside McRae. In the end, around two dozen CAs were built over the next ten years. Farmers reasoned they could possibly sell onions all year long and increase their sales four times. They did triple their production of Vidalia onions. But most importantly, time would now be on the farmer's side instead of the broker's.

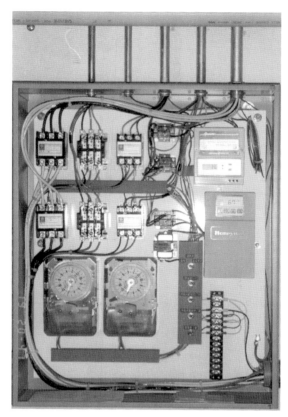

Left: Controlled Atmospheric Storage control panel. Includes thermostat, humidity control and defrost timers. *Andy Stanton.*

Below: Controlled Atmospheric Storage doors installed at Grimes Farms. *Andy Stanton.*

The introduction of Controlled Atmosphere Storage changed the Vidalia onion industry by lengthening the selling season. Prior to its introduction, there wasn't enough Vidalia onion acreage for the USDA to track production. The first records kept were for 4,700 acres in 1989. After that year, onion acreage increased significantly until its peak in 1997 at almost 16,000. Just like the farmers had predicted, there was room for four times as many onions. But after that year, production leveled off to around 10,000 acres annually. Farmers who invested in CAs planted twice as many onions as they had in prior years. Onions were available right up till Christmas for the first couple of years, but the storage costs and percentage of losses had taken a bite out of their profits. The Vidalia onion season finally settled out where they would be available through at least Labor Day in most chain stores.

Controlled Atmosphere Storage is still used today. Carbon dioxide has been replaced by ozone, and coolers are held at around thirty-four degrees. The rooms are not just closed but completely sealed. Rubber gaskets on the doors prevent expensive gases that replace breathable oxygen from escaping and letting the outside atmosphere from returning. The huge doors are held on rails that slide left or right, with a porthole in the middle of them to allow access to the rooms without having to open a door completely. During the summer months, when the onions are "sleeping," the doors can be bolted shut. Humidity is still a factor and has to be monitored because it will allow the onions to regrow and mold. These rooms range in sizes measured by the forty-thousand-pound truck load, usually holding well over one million pounds of onions each.

13

WOULD AN ONION GROWN ANY OTHER PLACE
TASTE AS SWEET?

W hat is a Vidalia onion? Is it an onion that is grown anywhere in the United States, as long as it's sweet? Is it only grown within the city limits of Vidalia, Georgia? Thankfully, but not without necessity, there is an airtight definition of the Vidalia onion found within the Georgia state law and USDA Marketing Order 955. The Vidalia Onion Act of 1986 defined the Vidalia onion as follows:

> *The Vidalia onion means all onions of the Vidalia onion variety grown in the Vidalia onion production area. Vidalia onion variety means varieties of Allium Cepa of the hybrid yellow Granex, Granex parentage, or other similar varieties. The Commissioner may limit the usage of certain varieties or authorize the inclusion of new varieties based upon recommendations of the director of the Experiment Stations of the College of Agricultural and Environmental Sciences of the University of Georgia. Only onions which are of the Vidalia onion variety and which are grown within the Vidalia onion production area may be identified, classified, packaged, labeled, or otherwise designated for sale inside or outside this state as Vidalia onions. The term "Vidalia" may be used in connection with the labeling, packaging, classifying, or identifying of onions for sale inside or outside this state only if the onions are of the Vidalia onion variety and are grown in the Vidalia onion production area. The standards for grades adopted by the U.S. Department of Agriculture, U.S. Standards for Grades of Bermuda-Granex-Grano Type Onions.*

Allium cepa is the scientific name of bulb onions. Allium is a group of plants that also includes garlic, shallots, chives and leeks. The resulting food is a yellow onion with a tan to brown outer skin, typically round and flat shaped. The flavor is sweet and mild, with a jumbo onion containing more sugar than a can of Coca-Cola. Vidalia onions must grade as a US #1, meaning it is of normal shape and color with no cuts, bruising or insect, animal or disease damage; #1 onions should be uniform in size and color, damage free and normal shaped.

Sizes for Vidalia onions are small onions with a minimum diameter of 1 inch and a maximum diameter of $2^{1}/_{4}$ inches. Medium onions are a minimum of 2 inches in diameter and a maximum of $3^{1}/_{4}$. There are no large Vidalia onions, only jumbos. Their size is a minimum diameter of 3 inches and no maximum diameter. Colossal onions have a minimum diameter of $3^{3}/_{4}$ inches with no maximum diameter as well.

For the last thirty years or so, retailers have simplified labeled fruits and vegetables using a coding system called Produce Lookup, or PLUs. Not only do onions have a PLU code of their own, but major U.S. onion regions also have their own PLU code. Vidalia onions are labeled with PLU code 4159 or 94159 for organic Vidalia onions. These codes are not interchangeable. No other onion can be a Vidalia onion or labeled as such. Many times, retailers have advertised onions from some other place as Vidalia onions. Every such incident can be reported to the Vidalia Onion Committee or Georgia Department of Agriculture to be addressed and corrected, no matter where it occurs in the United States.

Georgia has a greatly diverse agriculture industry, thanks to its three distinct regions: the Mountains, the Piedmont and the Coastal Plains. The Piedmont and Coastal Plains are separated by the Fall Line, what some people call the Gnat Line. Along the Fall Line are the cities of Columbus, Macon and Augusta. Between these cities and beneath the surface are large mineral deposits of chalk, kaolin and limestone. Underneath the soil north of the Fall Line is a solid granite base, which protrudes from the earth in one place east of Atlanta at a place called Stone Mountain. Below the Fall Line, the granite base layer is replaced with sandstone, which makes the Coastal Plains so productive. The sandstone layer plays an important role in the theory of why Vidalia onions are so sweet.

Sandstone is porous and granite is not, making it easy for some nutrients to leach through the soil and out of the root zone where it can't be taken up into the roots. It is surmised that the level of a nutrient that naturally produces heat and pungency in Vidalia onions is decreased with every rainfall in Southeast Georgia. One of the minerals thought to leach out of the Southeast Georgia soil is sulfur. It is an element used to make fireworks, flares and incendiary grenades for the military. As you can imagine, the less sulfur in the soil, the milder and sweeter the crop growing in it should result.

Several rivers cut through the Vidalia onion area on their way to the sea. The Altamaha River is the largest, formed by the merging of the Oconee and Ocmulgee Rivers near the Highway 221 bridge between Uvalda and Hazlehurst. The Ocmulgee flows from above the Fall Line into Macon and south through Hawkinsville and Abbeville. It forms the southern Telfair County border as it turns northeast into Lumber City before the merge. The Oconee River makes its way through Athens on its way south through Milledgeville and Dublin, splitting the distance between Glenwood and Mount Vernon on its way south. The mighty Altamaha flows to Darien carrying the drainage and silt deposited from its tributaries. The land around the Altamaha is mostly forests and saw many logs floated down it that were harvested in Middle Georgia during the nineteenth and twentieth centuries.

There are two similar short, small, southerly flowing rivers in the Vidalia onion growing region: the Little Ocmulgee and the Ohoopee. Loosely cutting a dividing line between Reidsville and Lyons is the big lazy creek they call the Ohoopee River. It turns every time it hits a cypress stump and deposits sand into the middle of the run, making nearly inhabitable sandbars throughout. Its headwaters are all the way above Adrian and never makes a sound or a ripple. Highway 280 drops down into a deep cut riverbed on both sides of the Ohoopee's run, giving the impression this lazy little creek was once mighty and strong, cutting through the earth for a span of a couple of miles. The whole run of the river appears motionless throughout, as though its contents are happy to stay put where they lay. The river runs the length of Tattnall County, turning just in time to miss the old Georgia State Prison. The river turns completely north and almost all the way around in some spots, creating shallow, sandy oxbows here and there before crossing through the settlement of Cowford in the southern end and dumping its sandy contents into the Altamaha River just above the Highway 121 bridge.

The Little Ocmulgee River is a much smaller river that receives its first precipitation from Gum Swamp Creek and then fills the lake at Little Ocmulgee State Park. The little river sneaks through and marks the border between Telfair and Wheeler Counties on a parallel course with the southbound Highway 341. It merges with Alligator Creek before dumping into the Ocmulgee River below Lumber City.

Both the Little Ocmulgee and Ohoopee Rivers run through very similar areas of the region, best experienced in the property at Little Ocmulgee State Park. Huge sand dunes are visible just outside the park's gates, including one that was once a popular obstacle for local youths to attempt to climb from the time the automobile was invented until it was wisely fenced in several years ago. Sand ridges and dunes are present throughout the length of the rivers' courses. The sand is so white, it gives the appearance of a heavy snowfall even in the summer. Turkey oak, live oak draped in Spanish moss and shortleaf pine appear to be the only trees that can tolerate the sandy ridges. The white sand ridges near the Ohoopee outside Oak Park are nearly identical.

The soil type of the Vidalia area can change several times in one field. There are loamy sands and sandy loams; the name depends on content proportions. Some of the fields where the original onions grew was pure sand bed, which is hard to irrigate but makes good onions.

The soil district where most of the onions are produced is called the Vidalia Upland. The area starts below the Fall Line Hills near Augusta and travels down to Sandersville and meanders toward Cordele and down to Tifton, where it follows Highway 82 and arcs up and around to bypass Baxley and Jesup to the north before pointing north to the Savannah River and back to its starting point above Waynesboro. The district is characterized by mostly flat farmland and forests. Throughout the district are veins of subterranean sandstone, known as Altamaha Grit.

About half of the Bacon Terraces around Alma, Baxley, Jesup and Screven are also present in the production area and are the only other soil district where Vidalia onions grow. The Terraces were formed as the ocean receded over time, creating terraces that are east-facing and grow shorter as they reach toward the coast.

After great angst and debate, in 1986 the Vidalia onion farmers and legislators finally hammered out the legal definition of the Vidalia Onion Production Area, which nearly covers the Vidalia Upland perfectly. It is described in great detail in the Vidalia Onion Act of 1986 and is described here in layman's terms.

Starting at the corner of U.S. Highway 441 and Interstate 16 near Dublin's Exit 51, the boundary follows U.S. Highway 441 to the southern Laurens County line. The Dublin Zaxby's at the interstate is out of the production area, but the new RaceTrac is in. Following Highway 441 from Dublin toward McRae through Cedar Grove, the east side of the highway where the Oconee River runs is in, but the whole west side and northeast portions of the county are out. The boundary follows the county line southwest when the highway crosses briefly into Dodge County to where the line crosses Jay Bird Springs Road, now designated as New Bethel Church Road when it ends at Highway 441 near the Wheeler County Welcome sign. The boundary then follows Jay Bird Springs Road south to U.S. Highway 341, south of Chauncey. The boundary runs right through the middle of the old Jay Bird Springs Resort, leaving half of the park inside the growing area and half outside. Using Highway 441 and Jay Bird Springs Road as boundaries was obviously to keep W.J. Grimes's farms in the production area since he grew onions only on the east side of 441 and Jay Bird Springs Road. The boundary perfectly cuts in the Grimes's farms in Dodge County, but not much else.

The boundary follows the western border of Telfair County through the middle of Milan and crosses Highway 280 and is marked by Telfair Line Road all the way to Highway 117 and continuing to the Ocmulgee River. Then, it follows the river along the southern end of Telfair County to the Jeff Davis County line. The boundary then follows the straight lines of Jeff Davis County around to the Bacon County line. It then follows the Bacon County line around until Georgia Highway 32 crosses it and the boundary then follows Highway 32 into Patterson. The boundary then turns and follows the Seaboard Coastline Railroad, running near the middle of downtown Patterson. It then goes north along the railroad tracks as it loosely follows U.S. Highway 84 to the west of it, through Screven, Jesup and Ludowici to the Long-Liberty County line, near a cement plant on U.S. Highway 301 south of Walthourville.

Then the boundary goes north along the southern border of Liberty County until it connects with the southern Evans County line, crossing Georgia Highway 144 east of Glennville, completely excluding Liberty County but taking in a small portion of Fort Stewart and turning northeast outside Daisy. Following the eastern Evans County line to the Bulloch County line, the boundary travels north along the Bulloch County line to the Ogeechee River. Then it follows north along the main channel of the Ogeechee River to the southeastern border of Screven County south of Oliver and on to the main channel of the Savannah River. Following north along the main channel of the Savannah River and to the Hampton County, South Carolina county line, but not including any land area inside South Carolina, it then turns west to a place where Georgia Highway 24 crosses Brannen Bridge Road. The boundary then follows Brannen Bridge Road and turns along Georgia Highway 21, in front of the Farmers and Merchants Bank in downtown Sylvania. Traveling west on Georgia Highway 21 to join Georgia Highway 17, outside Millen, it then follows West Winthrope Avenue through the middle of Millen, then west on Highway 17 to Georgia Highway 56 in Midville. The border of Emanuel County is followed south to Treutlen County until it is crossed by Interstate Highway 16, then west and back to the starting point at Exit 51 near Dublin.

After all that, there are thirteen counties wholly inside the Vidalia Onion Production Area—Appling, Bacon, Bulloch, Candler, Emanuel, Evans, Jeff Davis, Montgomery, Tattnall, Telfair, Toombs, Treutlen and Wheeler—and parts of eight: Burke, Dodge, Jenkins, Laurens, Long, Pierce, Screven and Wayne.

Promotion materials of the Vidalia Onion Production Area will all tout that it contains twenty counties in Southeast Georgia, completely ignoring Burke County. No one has any recollection of Vidalia onions being grown in Burke County, but there are several fields within the Vidalia Onion Act's described border between Highway 21 and the Ogeechee River when the borders are described at the point where the border runs through Millen toward Midville "thence westerly along State Road 17 to the intersection of State Road 56 and southerly to the northern border of Emanuel County," the area includes a strip of land in southeastern Burke County that lies east of Midville. A railroad line cuts into the landscape there, limiting the available acreage before the land becomes floodplain. The boundary turns south in Midville when Highway 17 intersects with Highway 56 in the middle of town, then follows the Ogeechee River west and then along the Emanuel and Treutlen County lines to Interstate 16.

Whole counties included in the growing area haven't produced a Vidalia onion in many years. Some of the clues that onions once grew in some of these areas are the road signs. Sweet Onion Road sticks out in Treutlen County, miles from the fields where they now grow. A couple of packing sheds here and there lay silent in their retirement, after making their owners plenty of money or not enough.

Along 441 from Dublin, there are signs painted with Rust-Oleum advertising the products sold at a large vegetable stand in a flat stretch north of the Little Ocmulgee State Park. In front of a large flat field where Vidalia onions once grew, a giant Vidalia onion that was built by local metal artist Charlie Grimsley once sat in front of the stand, which sells more Vidalia onions than any grocery store or market for one hundred miles. Down the road a piece, near Gray's Landing, another spray-painted sign advertises

Left: Giant Vidalia onion created by local artist Charlie Grimsley next to M&M Fruit Stand near Grimes Farms. *Author's collection.*

Below: Metter city mural painted in downtown across from the Food Lion. *Author's collection.*

Opposite: Claxton Rattlesnake and Wildlife Festival building with rattlesnake painting. *Author's collection.*

"Vidalai Onions Fresh from the farm," where twenty-five-pound sacks are stacked under a metal carport and sold on the honor system.

The best time to see Vidalia onions is in the spring. Right after St. Patrick's Day, the onions really grow and shine. If you want to see them for yourself, take I-16 to Exit 98 and drive south on Highway 57. It travels through Cobbtown, Collins, Reidsville and Glennville, the heart of Tattnall County's Vidalia onion country. The best places to see onions in Toombs County are down U.S. Highway 1 from Lyons to Santa Claus and English Eddy near the Altamaha River. Highway 147 travels along the river and crosses Highway 1 at English Eddy and cuts through onion country around Marvin Church. The community of Cedar Crossing on Highway 56 has lots of onions around it as well. The Woodpecker Trail, Highway 121, is also a great highway to take. The Woodpecker Trail travels through Metter and takes an alternate route through Tattnall County if you'd like to see the onions where they live.

Over half of the Vidalia onion crop is grown in Tattnall County with 4,833 acres grown in 2021, with a farm gate value of $69,595,200. Nearly as many are grown in Toombs County, with 3,987 acres grown at a value of $57,412,800. There are lots of onions grown in other counties as well. Usually, lots of sweet onions are planted within earshot of Interstate 16 in Candler County. Some 450 acres of onions surround the city of Metter, where everything's better in Metter.

One of the original counties in the conglomerate of Vidalia onion producers still produces onions but doesn't have quite as many growers as it used to. Montgomery County still produces plenty of onions, about three hundred acres. Since there's not a river or even a creek between Montgomery and Toombs County, the landscape and farmland is indistinguishable between them. Home of the Twin Cities, Ailey and Mount Vernon, Montgomery County is where you'll find Brewton Parker College. Down below Uvalda, toward the Altamaha River, there's a steakhouse called Benton Lee's, famous for a steak that's so big, if you eat the whole thing, it's on the house.

Onions grow in Bulloch County around Statesboro, home of Georgia Southern University, where people who are serious about their education go to school. (At least that's what my wife told me one time.) There were 726 acres of onions grown there, valuing $10,454,400. There are also onions to the south in Evans County, where you'll find Claxton, home of Claxton Poultry, two fruitcake factories and the Claxton Rattlesnake and Wildlife Festival, held every March. The festival used to be called the Rattlesnake Roundup, but due to pressure on the gopher tortoise, the roundups were discontinued. There are also about 400 acres of onions in Wayne County. Occasionally, you'll spot onions growing in small patches in Jeff Davis, Emanuel and Screven Counties as well.

14

THE VIDALIA ONION
AND ITS SUPPORTING CAST

THE GLENNVILLE SWEET ONION FESTIVAL

In 1938, the first Glennville Tomato Festival was held in town. It was attended by Governor E.D. Rivers and Agriculture Commissioner Columbus Roberts. At the festival in 1941, Agriculture Commissioner Tom Linder predicted, "Georgia tomatoes will be as famous throughout the nation as any product grown in any section." The commanding general of nearby Camp Stewart was always an invited guest at the festival. Companies of soldiers from the base were regular participates in the parade. The Glennville Tomato Festival was discontinued in the 1950s.

In 1977, the first Glennville Sweet Onion Festival was held. It was held at the same spots as the Glennville Tomato Festival but separated by nearly twenty-five years. The festival was sponsored by the Tattnall County Onion Growers Association. There was a parade downtown, a beauty pageant, a street dance and lots of sweet onions at the festivities around the Glennville State Farmers' Market. On the main stage at the market, Lieutenant Governor Zell Miller was the keynote speaker at the festival.

THE VIDALIA SWEET ONION FESTIVAL

Not to be outdone, the first Vidalia Sweet Onion Festival was held in 1978. Nowadays, the festival overtakes the entire city of Vidalia, centering

Above: Vidalia Onion Festival collage featured in Rural Festivals and Shows John Deere dealer calendar in 1985. *Author's collection.*

Far left: Coca-Cola commemorating the 1984 Vidalia Onion Festival featuring festival logo. *Author's collection.*

Left: Coca-Cola commemorating the 1984 Vidalia Onion Festival featuring original sketch of Yumion. *Author's collection.*

its activities on the Vidalia Airport and surrounding areas. Among the festivities are a Vidalia onion eating contest, an arts and crafts festival, a 10k run and a recipe competition. Recipes entered in the past have been logical mixtures, like relishes and pies. There have also been entries that came from way outside the box, like the Vidalia onion milkshake. In years past, Piggly Wiggly sponsored a cooking school for visitors to learn new ways to prepare Vidalia onions at the Sally Meadows Elementary School Cafeteria. There is a huge air show on Saturday of the festival most years where the U.S. Navy Blue Angels can be seen performing in the skies above. Country music stars have performed on stage at the festival, notably Sammy Kershaw, who was probably required to perform his song "Sweet Vidalia" there in the mid-1990s.

Bob Stafford

In 1993, after a career overseeing the produce inspections at Florida terminal markets, Bob Stafford supposedly retired. He recalled,

> *In 1994, the Vidalia Onion Committee asked me to come over and work on a compliance plan and help the committee manager with the experience I had. So I did that and after meeting several growers, I was just gonna be there for a short time, but I found the growers were some of the nicest growers and farmers that I had ever dealt with. I knew that they could use some of the expertise that I had. They wanted me to help them with some of the grading, labeling, and various other issues with the Vidalia onion. So over the next thirty years, we accomplished a lot of things and got the Vidalia onion on the very top of the sweet onion category. Right now, we are working with a strict US #1 grade onion and don't ship anything but a US #1. At one time we didn't do that but that's why we have such a high-quality, sought-after onion.*

As you can imagine, Stafford has seen a lot of positive changes during his time:

> *So many accomplishments, the growers came together and created a marketing order in 1989. Then in 1990, the Vidalia onion was established as the Georgia State Vegetable. In 1992, the growers got the state of Georgia to handle the Vidalia onion trademark. The Georgia Department of*

Agriculture was better able to protect it. That was probably one of the best moves they ever made by doing that. We worked really strong with the Georgia state legislature and established a royalty fund for the use of the onion's trademark in processed food products containing Vidalia onions, which is used for promoting the Vidalia onion and protecting it.

During his tenure, an important entity was created to fill an important role: "We found out the Vidalia Onion Committee can't do any lobbying and we needed to do some. We found out the legal way to lobby was by forming the Vidalia Onion Business Council. It was formed using the same directors the Vidalia Onion Committee used. We have a nine-member board elected by the growers."

In 2009, Bob Stafford was inducted into the Vidalia Onion Hall of Fame. After being executive director of the VOBC for several years, he was asked to serve as the manager of the Vidalia Onion Committee as well in 2018. He retired from the Vidalia Onion Committee after five years in early 2023.

YUMION

The most popular attendee at the Vidalia Onion Festival is a seven-foot-tall onion named Yumion. He was created by local artist Wayne McDaniel in 1980 when the Vidalia Chamber of Commerce wanted to create a character to use in promotional materials. Bill Ledford, editor of the *Vidalia Advance*, contacted him with the request. The original onion mascot was created, and a nationwide naming contest was held to give the Onion Ambassador a name. Not a local entry, but a woman from Virginia, came up with the name Yumion.

One of Yumion's first tasks wasn't an easy one. He had to travel into enemy territory, Walla Walla, Washington, and represent the Vidalia onion's interests at the sweet onion tasting competition. Word got back to Georgia that Walla Walla had held a tasting competition the year before and the Walla Walla onion won! The Vidalia folks didn't take that news very well and made sure the competition wasn't rigged the next year—the Vidalia onion squeaked out a victory. Yumion can still be seen at festivals and schools around the region. He is also the subject of a series of four books written by Rhonda Frost Kight and illustrated by Pam Alexander. Yumion is owned by the Vidalia Chamber of Commerce and lives in the Vidalia Onion Museum nearby. Opened during the 2011 Vidalia Onion Festival, the Vidalia Onion

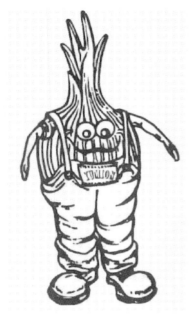

Above, left: Original version of Yumion created by local artist Wayne McDaniel in 1980. The Vidalia Chamber of Commerce wanted a character to use in promotional materials. *Ladson Genealogical Library.*

Above, right; Vidalia onion activity book. Produced by the Georgia Department of Agriculture. *Georgia Department of Agriculture.*

Left: Early picture of Yumion greeting visitors at the Vidalia Onion Festival around 1990. *Ladson Genealogical Library.*

Top: Yumion postcard. Modern version of the onion ambassador from the Vidalia Onion Museum. *Author's collection.*

Middle: Yumion the Onion Ambassador visiting Bleckley County Pre-K. *Author's collection.*

Bottom: Happy Birthday Yumion button created for spring 2020 advertising campaign by Erin White. *Georgia Department of Agriculture.*

Museum covers the beginning of the Vidalia onion industry, the history of the Vidalia Onion Festival and marketing campaigns through the years. The kids' play area even features a Vidalia onion grading machine that sorts different sized balls to show how an onion grader sizes onions.

The University of Georgia Cooperative Extension Service

Ever since the institution of the University of Georgia Cooperative Extension Service, its county extension agents have played an important role in the growth and development of the Vidalia onion, all the way back to the days of sweet potato farming around Johnson's Corner. Disease research and help solving pest issues have been important roles of the service. The UGA Crop Quality Lab offers onion farmers a test called the Onion Quality Package, testing pyruvic acid, lachrymatory factor and methyl thiosulfinates. Pyruvic acid gives onions their pungent flavor. The lachrymatory factor is what makes eyes water. Methyl thiosulfinates cause onion breath. Farmers and seed companies both use these results to make changes the next season. Limiting all three of these factors are critical in the production of sweet onions instead of just plain onions.

Vidalia Onion Research Laboratory on University of Georgia–Tifton Campus near ABAC. *Author's collection.*

In 1993, the impact of UGA Extension came into focus when a previously neutral disease threatened three-fourths of the Vidalia onion crop. The disease was found to be botrytis, a bacterium also known as gray mold that affects the onion through the neck of the plant, causing the leaves to turn brown and die. The problem was worsened that season because most every farmer planted their onions deeper than normal in response to the killing freezes experienced in previous years. The problem was also worsened by the unseasonably wet weather that year. Tattnall County Extension agent Reid Torrance was quoted as saying, "We've started planting our onions deeper to try to avoid cold damage. In doing that, we've initiated a problem with botrytis neck rot."

In 1995, the university opened the Vidalia Onion Research Lab on the Tifton Campus near I-75. $800,000 in Vidalia Onion Committee funds were used to build the facility, where long-term storage experiments were conducted to optimize the process and minimize damage. The head of research at the lab, Albert Purvis, stated, "It's possible to come up with conditions where you can have a Vidalia onion every day of the year, but whether that's what the growers want or need, I don't know. What I do know is that the growers need the prices stabilized."

THE VIDALIA ONION AND VEGETABLE RESEARCH CENTER

In 1999, the Georgia Forestry Commission closed its seedling farm on the Toombs-Tattnall County line near the Georgia State Prison and transferred ownership to the University of Georgia Extension Service. With the development of new seed varieties and new pest pressures developing every year, the university moved its Vidalia onion research closer to the growing region from its home base on the UGA Tifton campus. The Vidalia Onion and Vegetable Research Center was created at that time.

When a new onion variety is requested to become an official Vidalia onion seed variety, the plant has to pass three years of testing and evaluation prior to approval. Before the VORC opened, the seeds were planted on private farms or on the research farm near Tifton and then taken to the Tifton laboratory for evaluation. Now, onion seed variety trials are conducted in a secure environment, easily accessible to researchers. Bob Stafford explained the role of the center, "The Vidalia Onion Research Center, University of Georgia heads that up. They're second to none with that. They're working on different varieties every year because onion varieties will play out. So

University of Georgia Cooperative Extension Vidalia Onion and Vegetable Research Center sign. *Author's collection.*

Vidalia onions grow in test plot rows at the Vidalia Onion and Vegetable Research Center. *Author's collection.*

Top: Vidalia onions falling over, ready to harvest in test plot rows at the Vidalia Onion and Vegetable Research Center. *Author's collection.*

Bottom: Vidalia onion test plots plowed up at the Vidalia Onion and Vegetable Research Center. *Author's collection.*

you've got to keep up on it. We do it and the growers are really interested in it and involved in it. And in doing that, we've got an onion that tasted good, also. It's firm enough to ship but when this onion first started, it was so soft, it wouldn't ship. That's been rectified by a lot of research, time, energy and money. The growers have not only produced something to sell, they've produced something to eat."

In 2008, a new building was constructed on the property that includes an onion testing lab so that research samples don't have to be transported one hundred miles away for testing. Pesticide trials are also conducted there to evaluate compounds that can protect the crop from infestation and damage from weeds, insects, bacteria and mildew. Nine acres of onion trials are planted, evaluated and harvested each year, including every approved Vidalia onion variety and also white and red varieties.

The Vidalia Onion Banquet and Awards Ceremony

Starting in 1990, the Vidalia Onion Committee began holding the Vidalia Onion Banquet and Awards Ceremony. The banquet has a band, a dinner and usually a theme like the Wild West or Mardi Gras. At the dinner, the Grower of the Year Award is presented. The award "recognizes overall achievement and success as a Vidalia onion producer with an emphasis on quality production and compliance with the Federal Marketing Order." The first Grower of the Year award was given to Wade Usher of Lyons. Most years at the banquet, someone is inducted into the Vidalia Onion Hall of Fame. The award "honors a person who has significantly and positively impacted the Vidalia onion industry." The first inductee was Gerald Achenbach, first president of Piggly Wiggly Southern.

Another presentation at the Vidalia Onion Banquet is to the winner of the Courtney Wilkes Agriculture Scholarship. This scholarship is awarded to a high school student who is seeking to obtain a college degree in an agriculture-related field. Eligible students must reside in the Vidalia Onion Production Area. The scholarship is named in memory of Courtney Wilkes, a Toombs County teen whose family has been longtime contributors to the Vidalia onion industry. She was murdered in 2011 on the last day of her family's vacation in Florida. While vacationing at Seagrove Beach, her family made the acquaintance of a young man claiming to work for a beach equipment company supplying guests with chairs and umbrellas. Truthfully, he had worked for the company but had recently been fired because of his strange and unnerving behavior. He was also homeless after being kicked out of his house for the same reason. He talked Wilkes into taking a quiet walk on the beach when he lured her into a secluded area of the dunes, where he brutalized and murdered her. The family frantically searched for their daughter for hours, and the killer even pretended to help search for her. In the meantime, he boasted about killing the young girl and eventually showed the body off to a friend. The man was convicted of murder and is currently awaiting his fate in the Florida prison system, from which he will never leave unless in a pine box or a brass urn.

15

HOW TO GROW AN ONION

WITHOUT ANY TEARS

So, you want to be a Vidalia onion farmer? Well, the first step is to make sure your farm is actually inside the Vidalia Onion Production Area. If your place is inside the area, you may proceed. If not, you'll have to sell sweet onions or grow something else. As soon as your farm checks out, take a soil sample of your field and deliver it to the University of Georgia Extension Service in your county seat to be delivered to the soil lab in Athens for evaluation. When the soil sample evaluation report comes, it will tell you how much lime it will take to adjust the pH of the soil and how much fertilizer is needed to make a crop.

Vidalia onions are called short-day onions, meaning they grow during the winter. About three dozen varieties of short-day onions are available to be planted and marketed as Vidalia onions. Each onion has different characteristics, such as how fast it matures. There are two ways to get Vidalia onion plants: buy them or grow them. Seed plantings are done in September with a high-density planter. Seeds are started where one acre of seeds sown should provide enough plants for ten acres of finished fields, with population goals of about eighty thousand plants per acre.

When the plants are up big enough to transplant, the tops are trimmed with a finishing mower, similar to a lawn mower, to make the transplants uniform and reduce the number of leaves that the roots will have to supply with water in the early stages. Then, a plow blade cuts underneath the seedbed to lift the plants out of the ground. The plants are then rubber banded into bundles of fifty to one hundred and taken to the field in boxes.

Like other crops, the field is prepared by plowing and harrowing, but another step is added in. A rototiller is used to till up the soil and chop up field debris to prepare it for the plantings. Behind the rototiller is a custom-made piece of equipment unique to onion farming called a pegger. It is a steel wheel with pieces of rod welded onto the outside of the rim. Onion farmers in Southeast Georgia use them to plant a uniform field with the proper depth and spacing of two inches deep, four to six inches apart, and rows that are twelve inches wide. A pegger has a steel wheel that rolls through the field with "pegs" welded on it that make two-inch-deep holes at exactly the right spacing. Peggers have also been used by onion farmers in Georgia since before tractors were available. Proper spacing is required so the onions will get enough water and nutrients without growing into each other and becoming misshapen. Where each peg hole is, a plant is placed in it by hand, then the dirt is tamped down around it. Some of the workers who put the plants in the ground are said to be able to plant faster than you can walk while planting seedlings four across a row at a time. Onions could be planted directly in the field by seeding, but using plants instead is said to be more profitable and worth the risk. Even if a farmer loses a stand of onions to a freeze or something else, the field is still replanted by hand.

Onion planting is labor intensive. With ten thousand acres to be planted by hand, it requires a lot of workers. Planting is done in two stages so that all the onions won't be ready at the exact same time. The first planting begins about Halloween, with the last stage finishing by Christmas.

Georgia grows the best, sweetest onions because of its mild climate and adequate rainfall. The mild climate and rainfall also bring with them disease pressure that isn't seen in other short-day onion growing regions. Insects and weeds don't bother onions that much in the winter. When the onions begin to grow in early February, thrips will begin to attack them. Thrips are small insects that attack plants in large quantities. There are three types of thrips: tobacco, western flower and onion. The biggest problem caused by thrips is their bite is usually laced with a plant-killing disease. In 2020, thrips attacked large acreages of onions and injected the outside layers with a necrotic bacterium that killed the layer. New layers grew and covered the damage to make the onions appear healthy and normal. Once cut into, the damage was revealed. Chemicals to control thrips couldn't be applied due to monsoon-level rainfall at the same time.

The most damaging disease in onions is downy mildew. Because of the high humidity in Georgia, downy mildew feeds off the moisture, and if it isn't monitored, it can appear in one corner of a field and completely

Direct seeded onions at Grimes Farms in 1990s. Onions have gone to transplanting since then. *Jimmy Grimes.*

Closeup of onion pegger wheel attachment in a field near Cedar Crossing. *Author's collection.*

Tractor pulling four-row rototiller with onion pegger preparing bed for transplanting. *Author's collection.*

Hand-planted Vidalia onion field freshly done. *Author's collection.*

Top: Young rows of Vidalia onions grow in a Southeast Georgia field. *Erin White.*

Bottom: Bulbs of Vidalia onions begin to form in the field. *Erin White.*

destroy it in a matter of days. It and other diseases like botrytis and center rot are all controlled by fungicides.

When early February arrives, the earth seems to begin to break from its winter slumber. Just like General Beauregard Lee, Georgia's weather prognosticating groundhog, the onions begin to actively grow. Farmers begin to feed the hungry onions after a long winter's nap with calcium nitrate. As the fertilizer is basically pure nitrogen, onions respond to calcium nitrate much quicker than treatments from anhydrous ammonium or ammonium nitrate. Two doses of nitrogen are usually all it takes to grow onions to a marketable size.

In early to mid-April, the onions begin to give up on their struggle to touch the sun. As they reach maturity, the green tops of the onions fall over in the rows in a sure sign that they are ready to pick. The tops fall over when the nutrients and moisture in them leave to be stored in the bottom portion of the stem, forming the edible bulb.

Tractors with plows built to fit between onion rows perfectly run slowly through the fields, both undercutting the roots and gently lifting the onions

Left, top: Vidalia onion in the field. *Erin White.*

Left, bottom: Vidalia onions grow in rows near Collins. *Happy Wyatt.*

Right: Vidalia onions cracking ground in field. *Happy Wyatt.*

out of the ground and setting them in the sun to dry. Harvests must be timed correctly to prevent onions from sitting in the field too long because harvest crews can't get to them in time. These onions could be lost due to damage from rain, crows, frost, sun and just plain old Father Time.

After three or so days of the onions drying in the sun, harvest crews appear out of nowhere and begin to pick the fields clean. Each onion has to have its top and roots clipped off with a pair of shears before being dropped into a bucket. The bucket is then poured into a plastic bin box in the field capable of holding over one hundred pounds of onions. All-terrain forklifts pick up the bins and double stack them onto a flatbed truck to be taken to the shed. Around the first of the year, some farms begin an early harvest of immature Vidalia onions to be sold as green or spring onions.

In years past, the onions were plowed up and dried in the field. Then they were gathered in sacks and left to be collected and taken to the shed. They were then dumped into a semi-trailer or a hopper at the end of a grading line to be processed.

Above: Onion tops falling over in the field, a sign onions are ready to harvest. *Andy Stanton.*

Left: Onion tops falling over as a sign they are mature. *Erin White.*

After many years of trying, mechanical harvesting of Vidalia onions has never caught on. The reason for that is Vidalia onions bruise too easily to be harvested by machine. Several attempts have been made to perfect a harvesting system, including the same team that developed Controlled Atmospheric Storage at the University of Georgia Tifton campus. Even with the ever-present threat of a labor shortage, only one farm still relies on a mechanical harvester. Ray Farms in Glennville has used a Top Air Onion Harvester for several seasons. This machine picks over five acres of sweet onions per day, lightning fast if you consider the fact that most Vidalia onions are picked by hand; it takes about five people to pick one acre of onions in that same amount of time. The machine gently lifts the onions and "tops" them, meaning it removes most of the dried leaves and roots, leaving only the bulb. The rest of the unwanted dried material is removed

Above: Onions plowed and drying in Grimes Farms field. *Andy Stanton.*

Left: Plowed onions drying in the field. *Erin White.*

at the shed using a Top-n-Tail machine. The Top-n-Tail machine basically rubs and pulls the loose, dry skin from the neck and dried roots off the bulb.

The term *shed* can be deceiving. Sheds are huge buildings in the middle of nowhere capable of taking raw farm stock onions and transforming them into a marketable product weighed and labeled, ready for the grocery store shelf. Modern sheds today cover over an acre of concrete and contain modern processing and refrigeration equipment and marketing offices.

The first step in handling onions is to dry them down to remove enough moisture to prevent rotting. The neck where the top was removed is the most vulnerable part. The onions are dried for a couple of days or an entire week, if a rain came while they sat in the field on top of the ground.

Right: Rows of plowed onions dry in the sun. *Erin White.*

Below: Harvesting onions by bagging them in burlap potato sacks. *Andy Stanton.*

When the onions are dry enough to store, they are usually sized and graded. Then they are stored in coolers big enough to hold dozens of truckloads of onions. The same field bins that the onions are first stored in are used throughout the storage process. They have sides designed to allow air to flow through and interlocking legs. The boxes are stacked into dryers and coolers where they fit perfectly together, and propane-powered heat is blown through them to dry out the onions. The main objective is to dry the outer skin and neck to maximize the onions' shelf life.

Processing onions is fully automated. Onions are dumped at one end of the processing line, where they run across a grading line where workers check for damage and spoilage. These onions go to a #2 bin or a cull bin.

Top Air Onion Lifter combine harvesting Vidalia onions at Ray Farms near Mendes. *Author's collection.*

In-line dryers full of onions at Grimes Farms. Original design of dryers before the whole room design was invented. *Andy Stanton.*

Stacks of dried onions in wooden field bins under the shed at Grimes Farms. *Andy Stanton.*

Onion sizer on processing line at Glennville State Farmers' Market. *Author's collection.*

The #2s can be taken to a processing plant, where they are peeled and cut into a specific size. These pieces can be flash frozen or used in hundreds of condiments and products that contain the unique Vidalia onion flavor. There's no such thing as a #2 Vidalia onion, but these onions can be sold as plain U.S. #2 yellow or sweet onions, mostly for restaurant use. Cull onions are taken to a field and harrowed up or fed to livestock.

The #1 onions then run across a sizing chain or belt. The belt has several different size holes where the onions fall through and are sorted into small, medium, jumbo and colossal sizes. The onions are then bagged or boxed in packages of two, three, five, ten, forty or fifty pounds.

Farmers have learned to lengthen the Vidalia onion season by several months with the use of Controlled Atmospheric Storage. The perfect situation would be for a farm to sell half of its onions in the fresh market without having to put them in CA storage. These CAs use a lot of electricity and reduce the profit margin. Farmers try to sell their onions as soon as possible, though some sheds can stretch their supply until Labor Day.

16

IMMIGRANT VERSUS MIGRANT

A griculture is the business of taking a fruit, vegetable, fiber or animal and multiplying it into a marketable quantity. A bushel of corn planted on an acre of land should reproduce at least one hundred times that amount to be profitable. Quality judges the amount of return as well. Most crops produced have had advancements allowing them to be planted and harvested mechanically, reducing harvest time and the labor force required. Vidalia onions have had their share of research, but so far, no viable mechanical planting or harvesting solutions have been discovered.

To harvest onions in Georgia, it takes one worker to harvest about one-half acre per day. With ten thousand acres of onions needing to be harvested in less than a month, labor has always been the most expensive and precarious variable. Onions begin to mature and are harvested in the first of April, with the last onions harvested before Memorial Day, a period of approximately fifty days. If a major weather event disrupts the harvest, millions of dollars' worth of onions could rot in the field.

In 1960, CBS News Reports aired a program titled *Harvest of Sorrows* about the low wages and living conditions of migrant workers in the United States. Hosted by Edward R. Murrow, it changed the way Americans looked at agriculture workers. Agriculture was coming under the strain of two social changes. The baby boom had caused the U.S. population to explode while families were leaving the farm in search of higher wages and shorter hours in the city. With the increase in demand and loss of most of their local workforce, farmers gradually had to replace local workers with migrant laborers. These migrants were first U.S. citizens, some of whom were based out of camps in south Florida and the valley country of California. Whole families lived in barracks, in cars and under trees because they couldn't afford housing and daycare. Their children had to fend for themselves while under the supervision of their older siblings, some of whom weren't yet ten years old. The East Coast migrants in the report were loaded onto buses and transported to work camps in other states along the Atlantic coast as far north as Delaware and then back to Belle Glade, Florida, after the season was over. The pay for the migrants seemed small even in the 1960s, less than ten dollars a day.

Field crews were sometimes recruited from city streets and soup kitchens, preying on desperate individuals with nothing and lacking the education to realize they were being taken advantage of or finding a way out. Crew bosses would promise workers anything to get them inside a transport van and take them hundreds of miles away to work endless hours in the sun. By charging workers for transportation and housing, then gouging them for food, beer or cigarettes, crew bosses often had the workers in their debt at the end of the day.

Rules and regulations were gradually put in place to protect farm laborers, both domestic and increasingly foreign. In 1975, the first farm labor investigation was conducted in Homestead, Florida, by a former Marine named Dan Bremer. He came into the field where he suspected farm laborers were being exploited and unraveled the situation that the workers were in. At the end of the investigation, he asked the workers if they would like to leave. Forty-two workers followed his car out of that field and went home.

In the early 1980s, a bipartisan effort in Washington, D.C., began to regulate the foreign labor situation. Said Bremer,

> *We begin that in 1986 with the Immigration Reform and Control Act of 1986 that formed the I-9s that when you go to work for anyone in the US, they have to complete an I-9. That basically asks for identification of you and whether you are eligible to work in the U.S. In the legislation was one sentence, that said the US Department of Labor could regulate a guestworker program in agriculture in Section H2-A of the Immigration Reform and Control Act of 1986.*

Bremer owns a company in South Georgia that helps farmers obtain a legal H2-A workforce called AgWorks H2:

I was District Director US Department of Labor Wage and Hour Division in Atlanta, Georgia, and then in Little Rock. I formed this company strictly to help farmers bring workers under the H2-A visa program, and that's what I've been doing for twenty-five years. To bring in workers under the program and we harvest a lot of Vidalia onions, legally. Every worker that comes is legal. They don't have to look over their shoulder about anything. We pay their way up here. We pay their way back home. We give them free housing while they're here. We either provide them with meals or provide them cooking facilities. We make sure they have transportation to town and to the job and back.

Bremer explained the process, which is completely opposite of the version told in the news media. First of all, there is a difference between migrant workers and immigrants. A migrant worker moves from place to place, wherever the job is. Immigrants move from one place to another, sometimes crossing a border, but settling in a new place and not returning home:

The worker is required to go home and the employer is required to tell them that they are required to go home. The visa system is complicated, but the worker can stay for up to 3 years working on H2-A visas until they have to go home. The individual employer can only have the individual for 10 months. But the worker is eligible to transfer from one employer to another totally within the framework of that law. However, the paperwork has to be done so that the worker is under a certified H2-A contract at all times. The government requires that we fill out various paperwork to make that transfer possible so the worker can go from Florida to Georgia at a different time of the year. A lot of people do exactly that. They work vegetables in the spring/early summer and in July/August work watermelons in Florida for a different employer and that transfer is done through the Department of Homeland Security.

"The worker is in their home country. Let's say they're in Mexico in the state of Michoacan." Michoacan is a state west of Mexico City, about 750 miles south of the Texas border. This is where a majority of Georgia's H2-A workers call home. "They're there and they know when they are supposed to be in the United States. So, they are told the day they are to be at the Consulate at Monterrey, Mexico, the U.S. Consulate." Monterrey is one of the largest cities in Mexico, about 600 miles north of Michoacan and 130 miles south of the border crossing at McAllen, Texas. The U.S.

Consulate is similar to the U.S. Embassy in a nation's capital and run by the U.S. Department of State. "There are people there to help them with their paperwork. As soon as the paperwork is done, the Consulate will issue them a visa. At that time, they come here to Georgia to pick onions. Most of that travel is done on a bus. In Mexico, usually it is done on a Mexican bus company not licensed to operate in the United States. At the border, they switch to a U.S. bus company, and they come here. Some bus companies can operate in both countries. If we can find that kind of bus, we send it to their home in Michoacan. It takes them to Monterrey, then to Georgia.

"H2-A workers have to be doing agricultural work. It's easy to define, it's done by the farmer, on the farm or in the furtherance of that operation. So, they can be doing field work, tending, planting, harvesting. If it's the farmer's produce, they can be working in the produce shed packing up all that stuff. They could be employed to bring the produce to the shed, as long as it's on the farm. A lot of times, the packing shed is on the farm. As long as it's by the farmer, on the farm or on that farmer's operation, an H2-A worker can do it. What an H2-A worker can't do is work in a shed that handles everybody's stuff. It has to be 50 of that farmer's stock. Then you get down to farm labor contractors that do a lot of work on onions. If the shed is on the farm, they can work there. If not, they can't work there."

The process to obtain a visa must take place at the U.S. Consulate by the individual seeking to enter the United States. "Once they get to the Consulate and fill out their paperwork, it takes up to three days to be issued the visa. They have to stay in Monterrey or go back home then get their visa. I like for them to come and be available for the Consulate to question them if they want, and then when they get their visa, come on to Georgia. The visa is good for the amount of time of employment. It could be two months or ten or somewhere in between. The employer has their name on that visa and the period of time the employer told the government, the U.S. Department of Labor, how long they needed that worker. The employer pays for their way from home to the place of employment. They pay the bus fare, airfare, whatever. They pay for the hotel room to stay in Monterrey and, right now, its $14 a day to eat on their journey. The employer pays all of that.

"The employer pays for the visa itself. Its $190 per worker, and the employer pays that prior to the worker getting to the Consulate. The worker buys their own passport. A passport is a universal document in Mexico, and the rules say they have to buy their own passport. But, everything else, the rules say, the employer has to pay for."

The worker must have a passport and a visa to enter the United States legally to work. The passport is issued to the worker by their home country for identification. Their visa is issued to the worker by the country they wish to visit. Both must be obtained and kept up with by the worker.

"The governing bodies are the Georgia Department of Labor. They administer part of the program. The U.S. Department of Labor issues part of that program. The U.S. Department of Homeland Security has a part of the program. It then goes to the U.S. Department of State, which has Consulates around the world, wherever the worker's coming from. Whether its Mexico, Guatemala, Honduras, El Salvador, South Africa, the U.S. Department of State issues the visa."

While guest workers are in the United States, their employer must provide them with certain basic essentials at no cost. The employer cannot charge workers for housing, food or transportation to and from the jobsite. Because of previous situations, the employer could charge workers for these things with the workers finding themselves owing the employer at the end of the week, a form of involuntary servitude or slavery.

"H2-A and non H2-A is about the same thing. Non H2-A is subject to federal minimum wage of $7.25 per hour or if there's a state minimum wage, there's not one in Georgia outside the federal. If you are in H2-A, your minimum wage is the Adverse Effect Wage Rate, set by the United States Department of Agriculture, which at this time is $13.67/hour. That becomes the minimum wage for an H2-A worker. Now the farmer has to keep track of the start and stop time each day of the worker and then pay for all those hours worked during the day. At the end of the week, you take and add those up and multiple by the $7.25 or $13.67/hour minimum. You can pay by the hour or by a piece rate (by the bucket or acre, etc.), and if you're in H2-A, you're all in the same rule. If you use the piece rate, then you can make more than the minimum rate, but not less than, so you have to keep track of the hours, pieces done and how much they've made on those pieces to make sure they've made one of those 2 rates.

"The Immigration Reform and Control Act of 1986 instituted the I-9 program. The I-9 is a document that identifies the worker and identifies if they are eligible to work. So the cost to the employer, if ICE comes in and finds an undocumented worker and the employer has an I-9, they've looked and evidently it was false. Someone falsified the I-9, but how is the employer to know. So just to be truthful, the I-9 came about for the employer so they would have a safe harbor if they had illegal aliens and they'd falsified documents that they'd presented. If the farmer had those documents and filled that form out, they'd be held harmless. If you don't have that form and have illegal aliens at your place, you could be held liable and fined. If you brought them in willfully, you could be put in jail. It's a felony.

"H2-A can be very complicated. But if a farmer is paying the correct hourly rate and provides decent housing, the vehicles are safe. When they send their workers home on time, they're 90 percent ahead of the game.

"The biggest fine in H2-A is this: you didn't hire a local worker. If there's a local worker that wants your job, you have to give it to them. An employer must be leery of not hiring a U.S. worker that wants the job.

"It used to be they had to advertise in the local paper. Now you have to advertise on a website called seasonaljobs.dol.gov, and every H2-A job is listed on that website. So, wherever you're located, wherever you want to go, you look on that website and apply for that job online right there. If the worker is in your area, they can come to the farm and apply."

When asked how often and when the last changes occurred to the program, Bremer replied, "October 12, 2022. New rules went out, went into effect and we're living by them right now. They were subtle changes, not dynamic changes. Things you can and can't do. There are a lot of court cases and issuances that influence H2-A. You really have to study and keep up."

It may be no coincidence that Dan Bremer started his company, AgWorks H2, twenty-five years ago. One of the most contentious moments in the history of Vidalia onions occurred about that time, in 1998.

17

OPERATION SOUTHERN DENIAL

When the Immigration Reform and Control Act of 1986 was signed into law by Ronald Reagan, it contained a couple of pathways for citizenship for illegal aliens. If someone could prove they had been in the United States illegally prior to January 1, 1982, they had one year to obtain legal status. If someone could prove they had worked in agriculture for at least three months prior to May 1986, they were also eligible for the program. These individuals could be granted legal residence with the ability to obtain U.S. citizenship. When people traveled and worked illegally in the United States, records, names and Social Security Numbers were scarce or falsified. Applying for legal status had a deadline of November 30, 1988. After that date, rules would be enforced against workers without legal status and their employers, with stiff penalties waged against those who knowingly and repeatedly hired undocumented workers.

After the November 1988 deadline passed, an INS raid in El Paso, Texas, netted three truckloads of illegal aliens in May 1990. That raid produced a tip about someone hiring workers to go to Georgia and harvest Vidalia onions. In the raid, 110 illegal workers were seized and got everybody's attention that the grace period was over.

Though the Immigration Reform and Control Act of 1986 was law, not many farmers in the United States used the guest worker program. "In the early 1990s, a company in North Carolina started bringing in H2-A visa holding workers for the North Carolina Growers Association," Dan Bremer said. H2-A was seen as an expensive program that didn't line up with the farming operations in Georgia. After the H2-A program had been around a couple of years, investigators began slowly tightening up on farmers using illegal workers.

The fines started small and seemed to add a zero behind the figure every year, until finally on-the-farm raids became the norm. A May 9, 1995 raid in the Vidalia area produced 187 illegal workers. The farmers thought they were covered by state laws on the books, which they believed superseded the federal program. The INS leadership in Atlanta wanted compliance from the Georgia farmers, whom he considered were in a state of denial on the issue.

I asked Dan Bremer, "Do you remember Operation Southern Denial in 1998?"

> *Southern Denial was an initiative of the Immigration and Naturalization Service, INS. We call it ICE now. The person in charge of INS in Atlanta made a decree that he was "gonna be coming across Georgia like Sherman." He was gonna bring all his agents and they were gonna round up all the illegal aliens. Then, I don't know what they were gonna do with them. I don't know if they knew what they were going to do with them. And they put that word out. And putting that word out actually convinced some employers in Georgia to look at the H2-A program. Because they knew who was working on the farm. So, a group of employers started using H2-A and a lot of people didn't get into that. So, the Southern Denial had agents, helicopters, SUVs. They had unmarked cars, all gathered in Metter, Georgia, and they decided they would descend on a farm (near Glennville). So, as I was told by the farmer, the agents drove their vehicles onto his onion farm, running over his onions, squashing his onions that he had worked vigorously and very hard at planting. As they were making demands on them, he told them to leave. He stood right there in front of them and told them to leave. His brother called Senator Coverdell, and I think the president was involved and the standoff ended pretty much right there.*

That day, May 13, 1998, was the high-water mark of a running feud between INS and the produce farmers of Georgia. According to an article in the *Macon Telegraph*, there was a forty-five-minute period where agents and the farmers stood in a field of onions that weren't going to pick themselves. During the standoff, the farmers reportedly managed to contact Senator Coverdell directly, even with President Clinton reportedly being briefed on the matter by the end of the day. The INS agents had begun to detain workers, with the farmers realizing their irreplaceable labor force about to evaporate. Asked by the farmer by what right the agents had to trespass, one of the agents gave him an answer straight out of *Full Metal Jacket*. The workers were running, giving the agents probable cause to pursue due to their perceived admission of guilt.

Besides the battleground outside of Glennville, there were raids conducted throughout onion country over the next two days that netted about two dozen illegal aliens out of an estimated 2,500 guest workers. Similar to throwing a rock into a pond, the ripple effect spread throughout the area and sent most of the workforce, legal and illegal, into hiding. The general consensus was, "Congratulations. You got us. Now who's gonna pick the onions?" If the farmers were asked when the absolute worst moment to have an adverse event effect the crop, they probably would have said that week. If it was something out of people's hands, like a flood, fire or a giant meteor, they'd have chalked it up to fate. But this was the U.S. government, and it was about to ruin what was estimated to be about half of the crop still lying in the field. Not to mention this was the Georgia State Vegetable.

A series of meetings were called between the farmers and INS over the course of the week. Senator Coverdell and Representative Jack Kingston both sent representatives to the meetings. When reporters tried to attend, they were barred from the room or asked to get up and leave, supposedly by the INS leadership. During the meeting, INS attempted to get all the farmers to sign an agreement stating that they would provide housing, allow INS to inspect records and provide access to workers they needed to reinterview.

After the dust settled, the only signed letter was one that appeared on the desks of USDA secretary Dan Glickman, Labor Secretary Alexis Herman, and Attorney General Janet Reno. It was written by Georgia congressman Saxby Chambliss and signed by Senator Paul Coverdell and Representatives Charlie Norwood and Sanford Bishop expressing outrage at the "apparent lack of regard for the farmers in this situation and the intimidation tactics being employed by federal officials."

On Saturday morning, Senator Coverdell traveled to Georgia and held a meeting with onion farmers and INS officials at the courthouse in Lyons. He told reporters, "Farmers are relieved for the short term because they aren't left with a perishing crop." Later he chided the INS, "These outrageous bully tactics should not be repeated, and I have asked INS to change the way in which it conducts its raids. This is the traditional mess committed by federal law that's regulated by people who do not understand what's going on."

On Tuesday night, the farmers and INS officials again met, this time at the Shoney's Inn on Highway 280. The two sides promised to finally sign the agreement hammered out the week before. For reasons unknown, the agreement went unsigned and was eventually kicked down the road until June 25, but with farmers continuing to use admittedly illegal workers. It's not clear whether or not the agreement was ever signed. But when June 25 came and went, the INS lost their biggest bargaining chip when onion harvesting was over and the majority of the crop was sold.

The next year, INS arrested twenty-seven illegal workers at the beginning of the season on April 14. One farmer stated, "Maybe they're just sending a message that they're not putting up with any illegals."

After Southern Denial, Bremer said, "The farmers promised to do better on hiring falsely documented workers. The agents haven't come back, and farmers have virtually all gone to the H2-A program for a totally, 100 percent legal workforce at this time."

The farmers were still on the lookout for visits from the government. At some point, the Immigration and Naturalization Service purchased two custom-made buses from the Blue Bird Bus Company in Fort Valley, Georgia. It was mandatory for the company to run new buses through a shakedown on a predetermined twenty-three-mile road test. When the two green and white buses, with United States Immigration and Naturalization Service painted on the side, rolled off the assembly line, they were taken out on their test run, which only took about half an hour to complete. Before the buses returned to the Blue Bird plant, word had spread in Vidalia onion country that there were two buses full of INS agents headed their way. This was before cellphones, too.

TOMMY BUTLER,

THE SMALLEST VIDALIA ONION FARMER

O n the back way from Eastman to Dublin, there sits the smallest Vidalia onion farm of them all. In the shadow of Mount Carmel Baptist Church is Tommy Butler's onion patch. Two and a half acres of onions grow from November till May in a field between the church and Butler's house. He's got the smallest plot and the smallest tractor, and since he's ten or fifteen miles west of Highway 441 in Laurens County, he's also the only person outside the Vidalia Onion Production Area allowed to grow Vidalia onions anymore. I went to see him one day to find out how he grew his onions and his business.

He was born on the farm where he now lives, where his father was a sharecropper for the owner of the land, Butler's uncle. In 1958, his father purchased the land but had a heart attack and had to sell it six years later. Tommy stepped up and bought the farm from his father and continued on working the land. "In 1983, I bought some onion plants from Black's Seed Store. I planted four rows in my garden. They were big, sweet onions. I just used them and gave them to my neighbors. Every year, I'd plant four to eight rows in my garden, about two hundred feet long. I'd give them to neighbors and my family. In 1986, the law was passed with the designated area that starts in Dublin and follows 441 south to Jay Bird Springs Road, then it loops around Glennville and the Statesboro area. The law said if you were outside the designated area and had grown them for three years prior to the law, you could get grandfathered in. I applied for the grandfather clause and eventually I was approved after they came back and asked me some information. I gathered the information they'd requested up. They came out, tested my soil and looked at it, and came back. And eventually, it took about four months, I was approved. I got authorization to grow Vidalia onions and call them as Vidalia onions. The only problem with being grandfathered in is, if I skip a year, I lose my certification. So, I've been growing them ever since."

In an interview with *Onion World* magazine in 2015, Butler told of how he became a certified Vidalia onion grower: "At first I couldn't sell them as Vidalia onions because I wasn't in the right area; to be a true Vidalia onion grower, you need to be located within specific geographic borders. So, for a few years I had to sell them as 'Sweet Onions,' which was accurate enough because they are sweet. That changed when the Georgia General Assembly passed a law designating an official area that Vidalia onions could be grown, and I was able to officially label them as Vidalia onions. I've been a certified Vidalia Onion Grower since 1986.

"I started off with a half an acre and the most I've grown was 3 and a half acres. But now, since I've aged a little bit since then, I've cut it back to two and a half. I do fundraisers with 4-H clubs. I've done a couple of high school bands that have sold them as fundraisers. The biggest band buys a thousand 10-pound bags. That's the most they've sold, and their least amount was around 500, usually between 500 and a thousand 10-pound bags. Then I have another high school band that does them that sells about 200 10-pound bags and the 4-H club here in Laurens County sells them as fundraisers. The rest goes to local grocery stores. I have the local Piggly Wiggly in Dublin that buys all of theirs from me until mine are gone and they've been doing that for quite a few years. The produce stands, and then I ship them all across the United States. I've shipped from Maine to California.

"I had a guy called me one day and said he'd been ordering them off the internet. He said the onions weren't quite sweet as he thought they ought to be, so I told him to give me your address and I'll send you a 10-pound bag of onions. If they're not sweet like you like them, you don't owe me anything. But if you like them and they're sweet to your taste, I'd appreciate you buying them from me. So, I shipped him a 10-pound box, and about a week later, I got a phone call saying, 'My friend, those are the sweetest onions I've ever eaten, and you've got a customer for life.' So ever since then, that's probably been ten years ago, I ship him a 25-pound box at the beginning of the season and every two weeks, I ship him a 10-pound box. And the agreement is, when the onions are just about gone, I ship him another 25-pound box. So, I usually ship him about six boxes a year. The same thing goes for a guy in

Above: Onion grading table at Tommy Butler's farm. *Tommy Butler.*

Left: Tommy Butler ten-pound Vidalia onion bag. *Author's collection.*

California, I ship him some every year. I've shipped them anywhere from the east coast to the west coast."

As small a farm as Tommy Butler has, he still struggles with some of the same problems as the big farms. One of his biggest headaches is labor. "Its beginning where last year I had some trouble with help. The people I had used to help me plant and gather promising me that they'd come, and they didn't come. Then they were gonna come the next day, then the next day. So I called them and asked if there was a problem and they said, 'Yes, the people coming across the border now are getting free money and don't want to work.' So now I've contracted with some people that our local county extension agent sent me a list of three names that planted for the bigger growers in the Vidalia area. So, I contacted them and contracted with them to plant and harvest for me. So, I guess I'll continue to plant some as long as my health is good, and I can get the help."

Mr. Butler still uses local folks to help grade and bag his onions. His farm is also a popular local place to get onions. "I had three boys that started with me when they were thirteen years old and they're now in their mid-twenties. Their parents had to bring them when they started with me. They've worked with me since then, through high school. Then on weekends in college, they'd come help me. So, as long as I can get local help to grade them and bag them, I'm gonna try to keep growing as long as I'm healthy. I just enjoy the people, meeting the people I've dealt with over the years, and the people that see the sign hanging beside the road. They'll come and pull in at the shelter and buy a five-pound bag or a ten-pound bag. Some of them will get ten or fifteen bags, saying, 'I'm gonna take some to my neighbors.' I just enjoy growing them and dealing with the people I deal with."

Irrigating Vidalia onion patch with an irrigation traveler. *Tommy Butler.*

Left: Tommy Butler Farms Vidalia Onion sign. *Author's collection.*

Right: Stack of Tommy Butler's onions with grandbaby posed on stack. *Tommy Butler.*

Selling two and a half acres of onions, about eighty thousand pounds of onions, can still take a while to go through. "I've had them all the way till August. But when the heat and humidity get up, you've got to be careful. We hand grade them to make sure the necks aren't soft. We feed the bad ones to the cows. They know when that machine cranks up, they come running and stand and eat them as long as you throw them over the fence."

His equipment is different than anything you'll find on other onion farms in the state. "I've got an 826 International that I use to plant with, and I've got a 4430 John Deere. I have to take the duals off to use it. But I use it from time to time. I break the land, harrow it, fertilize it, lime it, etc. in preparation. Then I have a two-row cultivator that I removed all the feet except the trail wheel and put a twenty-inch potato shovel on it to lay off the rows. Then I've got a rototiller that I've mounted a bar across it. I had a machine shop to make sixteen-inch wheels out of steel that are about five inches wide. Then I've got a one-inch bar that they cut off and ground to a point and welded it onto that wheel. So, tip to tip, they are five inches apart and I've got four of them behind that rototiller. So, I've got four rows between the tractor tires so I can go along and fluff the bed, work it up, smooth it, then these wheels come along behind it and punch the holes five inches apart. So, it's got twelve inches between each row and there's four rows. So, it takes about eighty thousand plants per acre.

"I usually plant between November first and the fifteenth when the plants are ready to go. I usually try to use the earlier plants. The ones I used a long time ago which was Sapelo Sweet and Sweet Caroline, those types. When the tops would fall over, that's an indication that the plants were mature. The newer varieties, like Vidora, they don't fall over like the old ones so you have to go out there and make sure they're not splitting. If they're beginning to split at the root, then they're ready to come up. I try to catch them before then, because if it splits, then that's a cull onion and you can't sell it."

Butler relies on the Laurens County UGA Cooperative Extension Service to help him with his onions. A soil sample prior to planting is taken to determine if he needs to lime his field to adjust the pH and find the right mixture and amount of fertilizer to use. He usually starts out with a dose of 5-10-15 followed by one of 10-10-10 in the early part of the growing season. In mid-February, he fertilizes the plot with calcium nitrate, which is pure nitrogen, and then again in early March, for strong onion growth.

In order to plow up his onions in the spring, he uses a repurposed peanut inverter. "I took an old peanut plow and took the chains that took the peanuts and lifted them up and dropped them back down. I took and cut the back end of it off, the chain part. Then I took the motor grader, road machine blade moldboard and cut them. I left the shanks that the peanut blades bolted to and cut the road machine blade to be the full length of the plow and welded it to the frame. Then, I cut another one to stick in the bolt holes in the front and then I took the third ones, and when that one wears out, I can just cut the bolts out and get another motor grader blade. I take that same old 826 International and it plows them up and lifts them out of the ground. The onions just slide right over that moldboard and sets them back on the ground."

Mr. Butler has also had struggles with weather, insects and diseases in his plants. "In 1996, in March it dropped down to fourteen degrees. They were up probably eighteen inches tall. They were pretty plants. That was Friday or Saturday morning, and it never got above thirty-two on Saturday or Sunday. It dropped down to eighteen, and it looked like it snowed. It knocked them down. They were laying on the ground. I didn't know what to do with them. It was time to fertilize them. It was time to spray them. The only thing I knew to do was go on ahead and do what I would normally do.

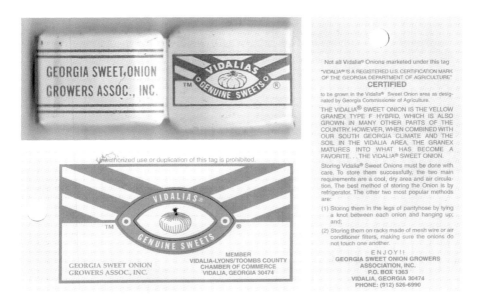

Left, top: Georgia Sweet Onion Growers Association bag seal used to prevent fraudulent onions. *Tommy Butler.*

Left, bottom: Certified Vidalia onion tag distributed by the Sweet Onion Growers Association affixed to Vidalia onion bags to guarantee genuine Vidalia onions. *Tommy Butler.*

Right: Back side of Certified Vidalia onion tag distributed by the Sweet Onion Growers Association containing storage tips. *Tommy Butler.*

Within two weeks' time, those things were back up and you couldn't see a brown spot on them. It was probably the best quality that I'd ever had. They just didn't have time to rebound in size, so there were smaller onions that year. I've had the same thing happen this year, it happened at Christmas, and they hadn't been planted but a month, and they're back. But they're just not as pretty as I think they ought to be this time of year."

At some point, Tommy Butler was part of the Georgia Sweet Onion Growers Association, which distributed tags and metal clips to place on the onion bags to prove their authenticity. The tags not only protected against fraudsters but also gave several tips on how best to store the onions. Still asked about today, one of the most popular storage techniques is described on the back of the tag: storing them in a pair of panty hose then tying them up to stay dry and cool. The technique was so popular that one of the associations bought cases of panty hose to be given out to customers so they could properly store their onions.

In 2006, Emmett Reynolds stopped growing Vidalia onions in Crisp County. His wife had died prior to the planting season, so he contacted the Georgia Department of Agriculture to let them know he was unable to continue farming them. In 2017, Robert Dix of Ocilla died after growing several acres of Vidalia's every year since 1986. That left Tommy Butler as the last Vidalia onion grower outside the Vidalia Onion Production Area.

VIDALIA ONION RECIPES

Honey-Baked Vidalia Onions
Honey makes the onions even sweeter

Yield: 12 servings

6 medium Vidalia onions
1 ½ cups tomato juice
1 ½ cups water
3 tablespoons butter, melted
6 teaspoons honey

Preheat oven to 325°. Peel and trim onions, cut in half and place in a buttered 13 x 9-inch baking dish. Combine remaining ingredients and pour over onions. Bake for 1 hour or until tender.

Sharon Davis
Fayetteville, Georgia

Marinated Vidalia Onion and Cucumber Salad
Kidney beans are an addition to this old favorite

Yield: 10 servings

2 medium Vidalia onions, sliced thin
3 large cucumbers, sliced thin, with peel left on
1 (16-ounce) can red kidney beans, rinsed and drained

Dressing

½ teaspoon salt (optional)
1 teaspoon sugar
1 tablespoon Italian seasoning
1 teaspoon fresh parsley, chopped fine
1 tablespoons olive oil
1 cup vinegar
1 cup water

In large bowl, combine onions, cucumbers and kidney beans. Toss together, separating onion rings. Set aside. In small jar with tight-fitting lid, combine dressing ingredients. Shake well; refrigerate for 30 minutes. Pour dressing over vegetable mixture. Refrigerate 2 hours and serve.

Carol Nalley
Atlanta, Georgia

Georgia-Grown Stir Fry
Carrots add great color and crunch!

Yield: 6 servings

2 pounds chicken breasts
2 jumbo Vidalia onions
4 tablespoons cooking oil
1 pound carrots
2 zucchini squash

1 pound yellow squash
2–3 ribs celery
¾ pound mushrooms
½ pound snow peas (may use frozen)
2 packages stir fry seasoning
Lemon pepper seasoning

Dice chicken and vegetables. Heat oil in large, deep skillet or wok. Sauté chicken and carrots until chicken is done. Add remaining vegetables. Prepare stir fry seasoning packages according to package directions. Add to vegetables, along with lemon pepper seasoning. Stir until vegetables are tender.

Sherry Cooler
Albany, Georgia

Vidalia Onion Pie Supreme
1978 Vidalia Onion Festival winner

Yield: 6–8 servings

3 cups thinly sliced Vidalia onions
3 tablespoons melted butter
1 deep-dish pie shell, baked
½ cup milk
1 ½ cups sour cream
1 teaspoon salt
2 eggs, beaten
3 tablespoons flour
4 bacon strips, fried crisp

Preheat oven to 325°. Cook onion in butter until lightly browned. Spoon into pie shell. In medium bowl, combine milk, sour cream, salt, eggs and flour. Mix well and pour over onion mixture. Top with bacon. Bake for 30 minutes or until firm in the center.

Mrs. Franklin Conner
Vidalia, Georgia

Vidalia Onion Cheese Supper Bread
An easily prepared complement to any meal

Yield: 8 servings

½ cup chopped Vidalia onion
2 tablespoons vegetable oil
I egg, beaten
½ cup milk
I ½ cups biscuit mix
I cup grated sharp Cheddar cheese, divided
2 tablespoons parsley flakes
2 tablespoons butter, melted

Preheat oven to 400°. Sauté onion in oil until tender but not brown. Combine egg and milk; add to biscuit mix and stir just until moistened. Add onion, half of cheese and parsley. Spread dough in a greased 8-inch round cake pan. Sprinkle with remaining cheese and parsley. Drizzle butter over top. Bake for 20 minutes.

Carolyn Crane
Stockbridge, Georgia

Vidalia Onion Dip
A secret recipe

Yield: 16 servings

3 cups finely chopped Vidalia onions
2 cups mayonnaise
2 cups grated Swiss cheese
¼ teaspoon Tabasco sauce
I cup grated Parmesan cheese
Paprika

Preheat oven to 350°. In medium bowl, mix onions, mayonnaise, Swiss cheese and Tabasco. Spread mixture into 13 × 9-inch glass baking dish. Sprinkle Parmesan cheese evenly over mixture and sprinkle with paprika to taste. Bake 30 minutes or until bubbly. Serve warm as a dip with your favorite chips or crackers.

R.R. Whipkey
Acworth, Georgia

Hint: This is a very rich dip and works wonderfully as an appetizer. For a lower fat version, substitute low-calorie mayonnaise and low-fat Swiss cheese and reduce Parmesan cheese to ½ cup. Result: One serving contains 124 calories and 7.6 grams fat (55 percent of calories).

Vidalia Onion and Pear Salsa
Great with grilled seafood, chicken or hamburgers!

Yield: 3 cups

2 cups chopped Vidalia onions
1 cup diced, unpeeled pear
½ cup chopped roasted red pepper (from a 7-ounce jar)
2 tablespoons chopped fresh jalapeño pepper
2 tablespoons chopped fresh cilantro
2 tablespoons lime juice
¾ teaspoon salt

In a medium bowl, combine onions, pear, red pepper, jalapeño pepper, cilantro, lime juice and salt. Serve immediately or cover and refrigerate up to 2 days.

Vidalia Onion Committee

Vidalia Onion Pie
Yield: 6 servings

2 medium Vidalia onions, sliced
1 tablespoon oil
1 unbaked 9-inch pie crust
2 eggs, lightly beaten
¾ cup milk
Salt and pepper to taste
1 cup grated Cheddar cheese

Preheat oven to 375°. Sauté onions in oil until tender (not brown). Place onions in pie crust.

Combine eggs, milk and seasonings in a small bowl; mix well. Pour mixture over onions in pie crust. Sprinkle with grated cheese. Bake for 40 to 45 minutes.

Vidalia Onion Committee

Vidalia Onion and Steak Salad
Yield: 4 servings

2 tablespoons chopped fresh parsley
1 tablespoon olive oil
1 tablespoon water
1 tablespoon red wine vinegar
1 clove garlic, minced
1 medium Vidalia onion, thinly sliced
¾ pound lean broiled steak, cut into 1-inch strips
1 cup sliced radishes
Leaf lettuce
1 cup crumbled blue cheese

Combine parsley, oil, water, vinegar and garlic in a small bowl, stirring to mix well. Set aside. Lightly toss remaining ingredients except blue cheese in a large salad bowl. Pour dressing over salad and toss. Sprinkle with blue cheese. Serve immediately.

Vidalia Onion Committee

Crunchy Green Beans with Caramelized Vidalia Onions
Yield: 4 servings

1 pound fresh green beans, ends removed
¼ teaspoon salt
2 medium Vidalia onions, thinly sliced
1 tablespoon firmly packed brown sugar
2 teaspoons vinegar (cider, red wine or balsamic)

Cook green beans in boiling salted water for 10 minutes or until bright green and crisp-tender. Rinse under cold water; drain and set aside. Cook onion in large nonstick skillet over medium-high heat for 15 to 20 minutes, stirring often until onions are golden brown. Reduce heat to medium; add brown sugar and vinegar. Stir to combine. Add green beans and heat 5 minutes or until beans are heated through.

Martha Wood
Conyers, Georgia

Vidalia Onion Pudding
Yield: 8–10 servings

1 tablespoon margarine
3 cups chopped Vidalia onion
4 cups broth (chicken, beef or vegetable)
1 (12-ounce) French bread baguette (8 cups bread cubes)
2 cups shredded Swiss cheese

Preheat oven to 300°. Melt margarine in large skillet. Add onions and cook until caramelized (about 5 minutes). Combine onions and broth, set aside. Tear French bread into small pieces; place in greased 13 x 9-inch glass dish. Pour onion mixture over bread; top with shredded cheese. Bake for 30 minutes.

Rosie Higgins
Lawrenceville, Georgia

Pork Chops with Glazed Apple and Vidalia Onion
Yield: 4 servings

4 center-cut boneless pork chops, ¾ inch thick
1 teaspoon vegetable oil
1 medium Vidalia onion, thinly sliced
1 large Georgia apple, sliced
½ cup honey mustard
¼ cup apple juice

Brown pork chops in oil in large skillet over medium-high heat. Reduce heat to medium; cook 5 to 10 minutes or until chops are done. Remove to serving platter and set aside. Cook onion in pan drippings in same skillet over medium-high heat for 3 minutes, stirring occasionally. Add apple; cook 5 minutes or until apple and onion are tender. Stir in mustard and juice; heat through. Spoon sauce over chops.

Paulette Korn
Dallas, Georgia

Favorite Fried Vidalia Onion Rings

No matter how high it's piled, a platter of Favorite Fried Vidalia Onion Rings won't last very long!

Yield: 4–6 servings

1 The biggest Vidalia onion you can find!
1 quart water
1 cup all-purpose flour
1 teaspoon salt
2 eggs
⅔ cup milk
1 tablespoon vegetable oil

Peel Vidalia onion; cut into ½-inch slices and separate into rings. Place rings in a large bowl of water; refrigerate 30 minutes. Drain on paper towels.

Combine flour and salt; stir well. Add eggs, milk and 1 tablespoon vegetable oil; beat until smooth.

Dip rings into batter; fry in deep hot oil (375°) until golden on both sides (3–5 minutes). Drain well on paper towels.

VIDALIA ONION GROWER

OF THE YEAR

1991	Wade Usher		2007	R.T. Stanley Jr.
1992	Adger Kicklighter		2008	L.G. "Bo" Herndon
1993	Raymond Bland		2009	Terry Gerrald
1994	Mike McKinley		2010	Delbert Bland
1995	R.E. Hendrix		2011	Alan Sikes
1996	R.L. Cato		2012	Ray Farms
1997	Delwin Dowdy		2013	Dry Branch Farms
1998	W.J. Grimes		2014	McLain Farms
1999	Jim Cowart		2015	Jason Herndon
2000	Edgar Wright		2016	Aries Haygood
2001	J.W. Beasley		2017	Omar Cruz
2002	Terry Collins		2018	McLain Farms
2003	James McLain		2019	Alan Sikes
2004	G&R Farms		2020	John Shuman
2005	Larry Powell		2021	McLain Farms
2006	Wayne Douberly		2022	B&H Farms

VIDALIA ONION HALL OF FAME

1990	Gerald Achenbach		2008	Earlie Jordan
1991	Tommy Irvin		2008	Doyle Smittle
1992	Charles McRae		2008	Mose Coleman
1993	Maxwell Smith		2009	David & Danny New
1994	Lindsey Thomas		2009	Bob Stafford
1995	Jim Bridges		2010	Delwin Dowdy
1996	Jim Hilderbrandt		2011	L.G. "Bo" Herndon Jr.
1997	Janice Grimes		2012	B.D. "Buck" Shuman
1998	Fisher Barfoot		2012	Gerrald Dasher
1999	W.J. Grimes		2014	Jack Hill
2000	Reid Torrance		2015	Dean Scott Angle
2001	Gale Buchanan		2016	Dr. Ron Gitaitis
2002	Robert Harris		2017	R.T. Stanley Jr.
2003	Ben Jack McDilda		2018	Roy Kreizenbeck
2004	Bob Redding		2019	R.E. Hendrix
2005	Raymond Bland		2021	Robert Meyer
2006	Bill Brown		2022	Bob Stafford
2007	R.T. Stanley Sr.			

TOP COUNTIES
BY VALUE—ONIONS

(USDA NASS 2021)

County	Acres	Farm Gate Value
Tattnall	4,833	$69,595,200
Toombs	3,987	$57,412,800
Bulloch	726	$10,454,400
Evans	576	$11,404,800
Candler	450	$8,910,000
Wayne	396	$5,702,400
Montgomery	277	$3,988,800
Wheeler	30	$432,000
Laurens	2	$28,800

BIBLIOGRAPHY

Chapter 1. There's Just Something About That Name

Coulburn, Keith. "The Onion You Could Fall in Love with." *Atlanta Journal-Constitution*, June 27, 1976.

Peterson, Kitty. "How Did Vidalia Begin?" *Vidalia Advance*, April 25, 1990.

———. "How Vidalia Got Its Name." *Vidalia Advance*, April 25, 1990.

Vidalia Centennial Memorial Book Committee. "As Sweet as Its Namesake: The Story of Vidalia." 1990.

Chapter 2. A Tale of Two Counties

Grice, Joseph T. *Sketches of By-Gone Days: Historical Facts of Tattnall County and Its People.* N.p., 1958.

Chapter 3. A Man Named Mose

Atlanta Tri-Weekly Journal. "Farmers of Toombs Make Money from Diversified Products." July 7, 1923.

———. "Pecans Sent Through Mails." December 1, 1923.

———. "Sweet Potatoes Pay High Returns to Toombs Growers." October 10, 1926.

Cave, Doy. "Historic Marker Signifies Birthplace of Vidalia Onion." *Vidalia Advance*, April 26, 1997.

———. "New Coffin Factory Goes Up at Savannah." *Columbus Ledger*, October 16, 1917.

Gardner, C.G. "Crop Conditions Are Fine in Lyons." *Macon News*, July 17, 1927.

———. "Farmers Saving Their Foodstuff." *Macon Telegraph*, June 26, 1932.

———. "Onion Crop Outlook Good." *Macon Evening News*, November 16, 1940.

———. "Plans Toombs Market Bureau." *Macon Daily Telegraph*, August 28, 1919.

———. "Potato Growers Pick New Officers." *Macon Telegraph*, December 18, 1926.

———. "Poultry and Egg Sale." *Macon News*, May 18, 1923.

———. "Poultry Industry Shows Increase." *Macon News*, May 20, 1926.

———. "The Story of Vidalia." *Macon Daily Telegraph*, November 30, 1919.

———. "Sweet Potatoes as Money Crop in Georgia Planted First in Toombs in 1921." *Macon Daily Telegraph*, August 31, 1928.

———. "Sweet Potato Crop Profitable at Lyons." *Atlanta Journal-Constitution*, August 1, 1926.

———. "Toombs County Fair Closes." *Macon News*, November 9, 1925.

———. "Vidalia Officers Elected." *Macon Daily Telegraph*, January 12, 1918.

Peterson, Kitty. "That First Vidalia Onion." *Vidalia Advance*, May 17, 1979.

Warthen, William D. "Unveiling and Dedication of Historic Marker Signifying Birthplace of the Original Onion Farm." Speech to Unveil Historic Marker of Original Vidalia Onion Farm, Vidalia City Hall, April 25, 1997.

Chapter 4. Ed Tensley and the Glennville Tomato

Allentown Messenger. "Crosswicks Blotter." February 11, 1937.

Cobb, Allison. "State Tomato Crop Lauded." *Columbus Ledger*, June 12, 1941.

———. "A Sweet Debate." *Tattnall Journal*, March 15, 2007.

Freehold Transcript and Monmouth Inquirer. "Advertisement." April 11, 1941.

Glennville Sentinel. "Many Million Tomato Plants Being Grown Around Glennville." May 7, 1942.

Macon Telegraph. "Glennville Ships Bountiful Crop." June 7, 1936.

———. "Program Completed for Tomato Festival." May 21, 1939.

Tattnall Journal. "Thelma Alston Tensley, 89." February 8, 2007.

Chapter 5. The Vidalia State Farmers Market and Earlie Adopters

Land, Will. "Vidalia Onion Crop Hit Hard." *Macon Telegraph*, June 3, 1971.

Linder, Tom. "Attention Onion Eaters." *Macon Telegraph*, May 23, 1974.

———. "Dedications." *Market Bulletin*, May 24, 1950.

———. "Farm Market Plans Finished." *Macon Telegraph*, September 18, 1949.

———. "Good News for Georgia Onion Crops." *Macon Telegraph*, May 16, 1973.

———. "Linder Visits Vidalia Market." *Macon News*, June 4, 1950.

———. "New Farm Market Opens in Vidalia." *Macon Telegraph*, May 19, 1950.

———. "The News from Vidalia Is Bad." *Macon News*, May 20, 1970.

———. "Onion Crop Hits Vidalia Market." *Macon Telegraph*, May 8, 1951.

———. "Poultry Sales Set Twice Each Month." *Macon Telegraph*, February 22, 1951.

———. "Tomatoes Are Shipped to Eastern Markets." *Macon News*, June 18, 1950.

———. "Toombs Growers Now Setting Out Onion Plants." *Macon Telegraph*, January 13, 1946.

———. "Toombs Onion Crop Will Be Increased." *Macon Telegraph*, December 5, 1950.

———. "Van Lewis Chosen Toombs Outstanding Young Farmer." *Macon Telegraph*, February 7, 1961.

Macon Telegraph. "Commercial Onions to Be Set in Toombs." November 23, 1955.

———. "Market Construction Nears End." January 16, 1950.

———. "Onion Discussion Slated in Crisp." November 28, 1954.

Chapter 6. A Southern Pig Meets the Vidalia Onion

Atlanta Journal-Constitution. "Piggly Wiggly Will Be Sold to an Investor Group." December 6, 1986.

Beasley, David. "Piggly Wiggly: GA Franchisee Bucks a Trend." *Atlanta Journal-Constitution*, May 2, 1984.

Grant, Tina. *International Directory of Company Histories*. New York: St. James Press 1999.

Macon News. "Personal Economics Course Set." November 2, 1973.

———. "Piggly Wiggly Makes Changes." June 29, 1975.

———. "Piggly Wiggly President to Speak in Macon Tuesday." September 16, 1960.

Macon Telegraph. "Thoughts, Talk and Speculation." March 21, 1988.

Norton, Erle. "Bruno's Strikes Deal to Buy Piggly Wiggly for $30 Million." *Macon Telegraph*, March 25, 1988.

Presley, Delma E. *Piggly Wiggly Southern Style*. Vidalia, GA, 1984.

Chapter 7. A New Venture for the New Brothers

Atlanta Journal-Constitution. "Advertising Notes." September 5, 1983.

New, Danny S. *Body Under Siege*. Bloomington, IN: 1st Books, 2002.

Chapter 8. Pirates Claim a Piece of the Onion Booty

Atlanta Journal-Constitution. "Onion Imports Bringing Tears." May 25, 1977.

Boyd, Bill. "The Onion Wars." *Macon Telegraph*, June 14, 1981.

Columbus Ledger. "Restraining Order Halts Sale of Imported Vidalia Onions." May 30, 1985.

Dwyer, Timothy. "Bootleg Onions." *Macon Telegraph*, June 24, 1985.

Fisher, Robert. "Onion Switch?" *Macon Telegraph*, May 22, 1977.

Hallman, Tom. "Firm Here Fined for Mislabeling Onions." *Atlanta Journal-Constitution*, July 12, 1985.

———. "The Great Vidalia Onion Stew." *Atlanta Journal-Constitution*, June 3, 1985.

———. "Judge Issues Order Against Scott Farms." *Atlanta Journal-Constitution*, May 30, 1985.

———. "Onion Scam Operators May Face Prosecution." *Atlanta Journal-Constitution*, May 24, 1985.

———. "Scott Farms Attorneys Charge Definition of Vidalia Onions Too Vague." *Atlanta Journal-Constitution*, August 8, 1985.

———. "Scott Farms Denies Any Role in Onions Mislabeling Scam." *Atlanta Journal-Constitution*, May 25, 1985.

Chapter 9. *Neilly Scott versus All Y'all*

Hallman, Tom. "Horticulturist: Genetics, Not Location Determines Onion Species." *Atlanta Journal-Constitution*, September 26, 1985.

———. "Vidalia Onion Labeling Case Returns to Court in Statesboro." *Atlanta Journal-Constitution*, September 24, 1985.

Market Bulletin. "Consumers Eagerly Await Harvest of Sweet Onions." May 8, 1985.

———. "Department Monitors Sweet Onion Crop." May 8, 1985.

———. "Department Satisfied with Onion Ruling." October 23, 1985.

———. "Judge Reaches Decision in Onion Rebagging Case." October 2, 1985.

———. "Produce Company Fined for Labeling Violation." July 17, 1985.

———. "Restraining Order Issued Against Onion Operation." June 5, 1985.

———. "State's Case Proceeds Against Scott Farms." July 24, 1985.

Tommy Irvin v. Neilly Scott, 1985003205, Bulloch County Superior Court, September 24–27, 1985.

Valdosta Daily Times. "Both Sides Claim Win in Vidalia Onion Wars." September 27, 1985.

Chapter 10. *Writing the Vidalia Onion Act, a Couple of Times*

Carlson, Carolyn S. "Officials Vow Quick Action on Onion Rules." *Macon Telegraph*, January 8, 1986.

Hallman, Tom. "New Vidalia Onion Law Defines Product, Stiffens Penalty." *Atlanta Journal-Constitution*, February 1, 1986.

Harrell, Bob. "Farmers Shedding Tears as Imitators Capitalize on Fame of Vidalia Onions." *Atlanta Journal-Constitution*, May 14, 1980.

Lundy, David. "Onion Bill's Originators Oppose Bill." *Macon Telegraph*, February 9, 1983.

———. "Suddenly, Everywhere's a Suburb of Vidalia." *Macon Telegraph*, February 8, 1983.

Macon Telegraph. "Panel Oks Loosened Rule on Vidalias." January 16, 1986.

————. "State Moves to Ensure Vidalia Onion Quality." April 7, 2005.

Market Bulletin. "Vidalia Onion Law Receives Approval." February 5, 1986.

Sturdivant, Camille. "House Votes to Define Vidalia Onions." *Macon Telegraph*, January 18, 1986.

Vidalia Advance. "Yumion Tag Registration Closes Here." January 27, 1983.

Chapter 11. The Vidalia Onion Grows Up

Atlanta Journal-Constitution. "Capitol Newsbriefs." February 3, 1990.

————. "Growers of Vidalia Onions Want a United Promotional Effort." March 8, 1987.

Bolt, John A. "Growers Want Panel to Promote Vidalia Onion." *Macon Telegraph*, January 9, 1987.

Columbus Ledger. "Onion Growers Want Shot at Vidalia Market." May 14, 1995.

Hallman, Tom. "Fate of Vidalia Onion Panel in Doubt." *Atlanta Journal-Constitution*, April 13, 1987.

————. "State Farmers Want Feds to Say Vidalias Are Georgia Onions." *Atlanta Journal-Constitution*, May 18, 1988.

Macon Telegraph. "40% Vidalias Sold Are Fake, Grower Says." September 21, 1988.

————. "Sizing the Sweet Spot." May 14, 1995.

Norman, Erle. "Panel Ok's Referendum on Vidalia Onion Promotion." *Macon Telegraph*, April 17, 1987.

————. "Plan to Protect the Vidalia Onion Fails in Vote by Georgia Growers." *Macon Telegraph*, May 27, 1987.

————. "Vidalia Onion Growers Want to Unite for Crop." *Macon Telegraph*, April 14, 1988.

Norton, Erle. "Georgia Growers Get a Sweet Victory Against Ohio Man Selling Fake Vidalias." *Macon Telegraph*, May 26, 1989.

————. "Supporters Claim Victory in Vote on Vidalia Onion Issue." *Macon Telegraph*, March 4, 1989.

Schanche, Don. "Sweet Onion May Become State's Veggie." *Macon Telegraph*, January 30, 1990.

Towns, Holly R. "Tifton Farmer Hopes Cry Heard on Vidalia Issue." *Atlanta Journal-Constitution*, July 13, 1995.

Chapter 12. How Mr. Grimes and Dr. Smittle Changed the Industry

Bentley, Cecil. "Stage Is Set for Annual Onion Feud." *Macon Telegraph*, February 20, 1983.

GA Ext Service. "Special Storage Extends Life of Vidalia's." *Atlanta Journal-Constitution*, August 19, 1984.

Harrell, Bob. "Banking Vidalia's." *Atlanta Journal-Constitution*, April 11, 1990.

Macon Telegraph. "Horticulture Comes a Long Way from Stump Pulling, Hole Filling." October 17, 1975.

———. "Nitrogen Tanks Extend Life of Vidalia Onions." October 31, 1988.

Walk, Jane. "The Vidalia Onion Storage Experiment." *Rural Georgia*, February 1990.

Chapter 13. Would an Onion Grown Any Other Place Taste As Sweet?

Gore, Pamela J.W., and William Witherspoon. *Roadside Geology of Georgia*. Missoula, MT: Mountain Press Publishing, 2013.

Chapter 14. The Vidalia Onion and Its Supporting Cast

Atlanta Journal-Constitution. "Onion Festival Set for Saturday." May 13, 1977.

Bynum, Russ. "Museum Dishes the History of Vidalia Onions." *Columbus Ledger-Enquirer*, June 18, 2011.

Columbus Ledger. "Fungus Threatens Vidalia Onions." February 18, 1993.

Lameiras, Maria M. "Soil Conditions, Fertilizers Affect the Sweetness of Vidalia Onions." UGA press release, August 5, 2021.

Minor, Elliott. "Napping for Science." *Macon Telegraph*, January 30, 1995.

Peterson, Kitty, and Cathy Harrison. "They Named Him Yumion." *Vidalia Advance*, May 14, 1987.

———. "Vidalia Onions' Kin a Fascinating Family." UGA Press release. November 25, 1998.

Chapter 16. Immigrant versus Migrant

Murrow, Edward R. "1960: 'Harvest of Shame.'" YouTube, Educational video, 52:05. https://www.youtube.com/watch?v=yJTVF_dya7E&t=18s.

Chapter 17. Operation Southern Denial

Atlanta Journal-Constitution. "Accord on Workers Is Delayed by INS." May 31, 1998.

Beasley, David. "Farmers Fear New Immigration Law Will Spoil Labor Crop." *Atlanta Journal-Constitution*, August 23, 1987.

Columbus Ledger Enquirer. "Immigration Officials Watching Onion Fields." May 21, 1995.

Davis, Jingle. "INS to Detain 110 Harvesting Vidalias." *Atlanta Journal-Constitution*, May 8, 1990.

———. "Vidalia Arrest Site Stuns INS Officials." *Atlanta Journal-Constitution*, April 16, 1999.

―――. "Vidalia Growers, INS Near Deal." *Atlanta Journal-Constitution*, May 20, 1998.

Jones, Gregory R. "Farmers, INS Talk." *Macon Telegraph*, May 15, 1998.

―――. "INS Raids Threaten Vidalia Harvest." *Macon Telegraph*, May 14, 1998.

―――. "Onion Farmers, INS Compromise." *Macon Telegraph*, May 16, 1998.

Macon Telegraph. "Coverdell Says INS Deal Just a Stopgap." May 17, 1998.

Montgomery, Bill. "Tough Immigration Law Changes the Way Georgians Do Business." *Atlanta Journal-Constitution*, June 19, 1988.

Chapter 18. Tommy Butler, the Smallest Vidalia Onion Farmer

Hind, Andrew. "Small Farm, Big Flavor." *Onion World*, November 2015.

Vidalia Onion Recipes

Alderman, E. Shaunn. *Seasons of Georgia Kitchen Keepsake Cookbook*. Georgia Department of Agriculture, 2007.

Brown, Fred. *The Best of Georgia Farms: A Cookbook and Tour Book*. Atlanta, GA: CI Publishing, 1998.

Payne, Susan Carlisle. *The Southern Living Cookbook*. 6th ed. Birmingham, AL: Oxmoor House, 1991.

ABOUT THE AUTHOR

Lee Lancaster works with the Georgia Department of Agriculture as a contributing writer for the *Farmers and Consumers Market Bulletin*. His "Georgie's Drive" is a feature about Georgia agriculture and rural history appearing biweekly since 2017. He also serves as a marketing specialist for Vidalia onions and coordinates the Baby Barn program at the Georgia National Fair in October.

Lee attended ABAC for only two years and then moved on to the University of Georgia during the Donnan era or Carter administration—Quincy, that is. In spite of that, he still roots for the 'Dawgs. When he was not attending football games, he studied agriculture and cleaned chicken houses.

His strong interest in agriculture comes from his family, which has been in involved in farming since Adam and Eve shared an apple. Granddaddy WD Knowles was thought to be John Deere by local children in Milan for many years when he sold tractors, combines and plows. The family has raised Polled Hereford cattle since the mid-1980s.

He lives in Eastman with his wife, Keri; two children, Nate and Caroline; and two dogs, Morty and Noodle. The family can be found at Siloam Baptist Church every Sunday and Wednesday.